UNDERSTANDING
Katherine Anne Porter

Understanding Contemporary
American Literature

Matthew J. Bruccoli, *Editor*

UNDERSTANDING
Katherine
Anne
PORTER

by DARLENE HARBOUR UNRUE

UNIVERSITY OF SOUTH CAROLINA PRESS

For
John

CONTENTS

EDITOR'S PREFACE

Understanding Contemporary American Literature has been planned as a series of guides or companions for students as well as good nonacademic readers. The editor and publisher perceive a need for these volumes because much of the influential contemporary literature makes special demands. Uninitiated readers encounter difficulty in approaching works that depart from the traditional forms and techniques of prose and poetry. Literature relies on conventions, but the conventions keep evolving; new writers form their own conventions—which in time may become familiar. Put simply, *UCAL* provides instruction in how to read certain contemporary writers—identifying and explicating their material, themes, use of language, point of view, structures, symbolism, and responses to experience.

The word *understanding* in the series title was deliberately chosen. Many willing readers lack an adequate understanding of how contemporary literature works; that is, what the author is attempting to express and the means by which it is conveyed. Although the criticism and analysis in the series have been aimed at a level of general accessibility, these introductory volumes are meant to be applied in conjunction with the works they cover. Thus they do not provide a substitute for the works and authors they introduce, but rather prepare the reader for more profitable literary experiences.

M. J. B.

UNDERSTANDING
Katherine Anne Porter

CHAPTER ONE

Understanding
Katherine Anne Porter

Career

Katherine Anne Porter's long life was divided into two distinct segments. Her first twenty-three years were spent in rural Texas steeped in Southwestern customs and informed with stories of the Civil War and family legend carried from Kentucky. She lived the remainder of her life absorbing experience outside her native region. Each part contributed subjects and themes to her fiction, and occasionally both functioned in concert to produce a unique stylistic richness.

She was born May 15, 1890, in Indian Creek, Texas, the fourth of five children of Harrison Boone Porter and Mary Alice Jones Porter, both of whose letters reveal a literary style and a familiarity with the classics of literature. Her mother died when Katherine Anne was two years old, and her rearing was shared by her father and her paternal grandmother, Catherine Anne Skaggs Por-

1

ter, who provided the model for the grandmothers in "The Old Order," "The Downward Path to Wisdom," and "The Jilting of Granny Weatherall." Porter's formal education ended at age fifteen after a year at the Thomas School in San Antonio, and her adolescence ended at age sixteen with an early marriage to John Henry Koontz, whose family introduced her into Roman Catholicism. When that marriage ended nine years later, she already had begun the preparation for her writing career, which would span the greater part of the twentieth century.

Porter's flight from her first marriage and Texas in 1913 set her on a nomadic course that led to Chicago, Denver, New York, Connecticut, Mexico, Bermuda, California, and Europe, with only rare visits to Texas. The years between 1913 and 1921 were marked by serious illnesses (tuberculosis in 1915 and a nearly fatal influenza in 1918) and apprenticeship writing. In New York in 1919 she met Mexican artists who made possible a magazine assignment that sent her to Mexico in 1920. Although the Mexico years, 1920–1931, were broken up by long sojourns in the United States, the years were important to Porter because they provided the experiences upon which she based her first original pieces of fiction.

When Porter left Mexico in 1931 for Europe, she had been married and divorced a second time (to Ernest Stock, 1925–26), and she was entering another phase of

CAREER

her traveling and writing that would solidify many of her political and aesthetic views. Before the Second World War ended, she had tried and rejected marriage two more times, first to Eugene Pressly from 1933 to 1938, and then to Albert Erskine from 1938 to 1942. In 1944 she moved to the Washington, D.C. area, which was to be her home base for the rest of her life. When she began to accept university appointments in 1948, she was struggling to finish her major work, a long novel begun in 1940. The struggle was to last more than a dozen years before the work would appear as *Ship of Fools*. Porter died in Washington September 19, 1980, and was buried beside her mother in the family plot near Indian Creek, Texas.

In 1922 Porter's first published story, "María Concepción," appeared in *Century* magazine. Until that time she had published retellings of known fables; she had done hack writing for newspapers in Fort Worth, Chicago, and Denver; she had ghostwritten an account of a young American woman's marriage to a Chinese student (*My Chinese Marriage*); and she had written a pamphlet (*Outline of Mexican Popular Arts and Crafts*) to accompany a Mexican folk-art exhibit to the United States. In 1930 "María Concepción" was among Porter's stories gathered under the title *Flowering Judas and Other Stories*, which in addition to the title story included "Magic," "Rope," "He," and "The Jilting of Granny Weatherall." With the exception of "The Martyr" and

"Virgin Violeta," the slim volume represented Porter's cumulative fictional work to that date.

The collection won immediate and enthusiastic praise from critics. In the *New Republic* Louise Bogan declared that there was "nothing quite like" Porter's talent, "very little" that approached "its strength in contemporary writing."[1] Yvor Winters, writing in the *Hound & Horn*, said, "I can think of no living American who has written short stories at once so fine in detail, so powerful as units, and so mature and intelligent in outlook, except W. C. Williams, and one can make that exception for but one of his compositions."[2] The critical success of the first edition of *Flowering Judas* fixed Porter's high position in American letters at the same time it earned her a Guggenheim Fellowship. When the collection was expanded in 1935 to include "Theft," "That Tree," "The Cracked Looking-Glass," and "Hacienda," the praise continued. John Chamberlain wrote in the *New York Times*, "After five years, the intensity of these stories seems just as important as it did when they were originally published."[3]

By the time the first substantial critical article on Porter's work, Lodwick Hartley's "Katherine Anne Porter," appeared in the *Sewanee Review* in 1940, Porter had developed the Miranda cycle, and her second collection of fiction, *Pale Horse, Pale Rider: Three Short Novels*, already had made its appearance to a still enthusiastic critical reception. Lewis Gannett called Porter one of the greatest American writers,[4] and Paul Rosenfeld said that she moved in the illustrious company headed by Hawthorne, Flaubert, and Henry James.[5] In spite of this critical praise, however, Porter's readership remained exclusive and relatively small, and throughout the 1930s, 1940s, and 1950s a disparity continued to exist between the critical adulation of Porter's work and her popular audience. Robert Penn Warren began his 1942 article on Porter, the now classic "Irony with a Center," published in the *Kenyon Review*, with a direct acknowledgment of the phenomenon. Porter's fiction, Warren claimed, had not found the public which its distinction merited. He traced the cause to Porter's refusal to compromise her artistic integrity for the popular market and to reviewers who in summarizing her work with phrases like "beautiful style" had unwittingly implied to potential readers that "exquisiteness" was substituted for substance and that the medium of Porter's fiction was more apparent than the artistic vision the medium conveyed.[6] The publication in 1952 of a collection of Porter's essays (*The Days Before*) allowed reviewers to expand their praise to include Porter's critical perception, but it failed to draw in new readers.

Articles on Porter's work continued to appear at regular intervals, and in 1957 the first book on Porter, *The Fiction and Criticism of Katherine Anne Porter*, by Harry John Mooney, Jr., was published. But not until the publication of *Ship of Fools* in 1962 did Porter's popular reputation catch up with her firmly established critical fame and bring with it long-awaited financial reward. In 1965 her popularity on both fronts intensified with the publication of *The Collected Stories of Katherine Anne Porter*, which in 1966 won both the Pulitzer Prize and the National Book Award. Her last major work was *The Collected Essays and Occasional Writings of Katherine Anne Porter* (1970), which included her poetry and a broad range of her essays, letters, and excerpts from her journal.

Parenthetical numbers in this text refer to the standard editions of her works: *The Collected Stories, The Collected Essays and Occasional Writings*, and the first edition of *Ship of Fools*.

Overview

Porter's works have defied easy interpretation and have presented unique problems to the contemporary reader. Several facts account for the difficulty, which prompted John W. Aldridge to declare that although Porter "remains the symbol and custodian of an excellence that is almost everywhere appreciated," it is nevertheless an excellence that is "almost nowhere clearly understood."[7] One cause of the difficulty has been the failure of readers to see a proper unity in her canon, and another cause has been an incomplete understanding of her stylistic techniques.

OVERVIEW

Although some readers have seen no logical agree-ment among the works (for example, Edmund Wilson insisted that Porter's stories were not "illustrations of anything that is reducible to a moral law, or a political or social analysis, or even a principle of human behav-ior"), other readers have argued for a comprehensive interpretation of her canon but have not been able to agree on what it should be.[8] Throughout her life, Porter complicated the difficulty by resisting dogma and at-tachment to aesthetic movements that would have placed her in recognizable currents of contemporary thought. Yet she left no doubt that there was a coher-ence to all her work.

In 1940, looking back on twenty years of writing, Porter commented that her stories were "fragments of a much larger plan," which she was "still engaged in car-rying out."[9] Later she praised Caroline Gordon's perspi-cacity in seeing a unity in all her stories.[10] What Porter called her "larger plan" is the motif of a journey toward truth about oneself and the universe. The progress to-ward truth is hard won, and relatively few of her stories contain illuminations. Although many stories contain representative trips, voyages, and excursions, Porter often subsumes the journey in a surface story that illus-trates the obstacles in that movement toward enlighten-ment. She identified as obstacles civilized men's and women's ingrained distaste for the primitive that co-exists with the intellectual in the human psyche, their grasping at systems, rituals, or romantic ideals as a sub-stitute for truth, and their failure to acknowledge that at the heart of the universe stands a mystery, the answer to which, Porter says, may be God, or love.

While all of Porter's stories and her long novel are loosely controlled by this general thesis, their multiple secondary themes reflect her topical concerns and particular experiences at the time of writing each work. Her early stories that are set in Mexico show her fascination with the primitive base of human existence and the way it reveals itself in ordinary life. These early stories also contain political themes relevant to the Mexican cultural revolution (1910–1936). Political themes are present in "Pale Horse, Pale Rider," "The Leaning Tower," and *Ship of Fools*, all of which are permeated with the prewar atmosphere of the 1930s. Betrayal is a theme that concerned Porter all her life and in most of her works. The power of love is also a strong underlying theme, either by precise illumination when she shows the horrors that result when love is withheld, as in "The Downward Path to Wisdom," "He," "Magic," and *Ship of Fools*, or when love is displaced, as in "The Martyr," "Flowering Judas," "Hacienda," "The Cracked Looking-Glass," and "Holiday."

The characters that act out these themes are drawn from Porter's wide-ranging experience, and most of them are intrinsic to their settings. María Concepción, for example, would not be the same character, with her special dilemma, outside modern Mexico. Other characters (the husband and wife in "Rope" are good examples) seem to defy association with a setting, their personal conflicts independent of a particular region.

OVERVIEW

Still other characters who are minor in a story's primary emphasis, exist only as details in a realistic backdrop. Porter's array of characters includes Mexican primitives, aristocrats, artists, and revolutionaries; Anglo-American expatriates; backwoods characters in Texas and New England; Scandinavian and German immigrants in the Southwest; rootless inhabitants of Greenwich Village; remnants of the Southern aristocracy spread from New Orleans to Texas; Irish Catholics in New York and Connecticut; and a variety of Europeans.

Porter's most important characters recur throughout her fiction and cross settings and times. Her autobiographical protagonist, an innocent female child or a naive young woman, began emerging in drafts of stories in the 1920s. In the seven stories that make up "The Old Order" (1935–1960), the character is named Miranda, and Miranda's rite of passage is explored also in "Old Mortality" and "Pale Horse, Pale Rider." Many of Porter's other central characters share some traits with Miranda, who absorbs truths about herself, her femaleness and mortality, about the inefficacy of systems and the illusoriness of idealism, and about the nature of love. These same truths concern Violeta in "Virgin Violeta," Laura in "Flowering Judas," Charles Upton in "The Leaning Tower," the unnamed narrators of "Hacienda" and "Holiday," and the unnamed protagonist of "Theft." In *Ship of Fools* Jenny Brown in particular and Mrs. Treadwell in some respects are the final developments of the autobiographical center in Porter's fiction.

UNDERSTANDING KATHERINE ANNE PORTER

The creation of the child Miranda in "The Circus," "The Fig Tree," "The Grave," and "Old Mortality," probably was inspired in part by the child characters of Henry James, as were He in "He" and Stephen in "The Downward Path to Wisdom." Porter admired finely drawn child characters, saying that James's children were nearly the best in all of fiction and praising James's understanding of the child as a stranger in an adult world.[11]

Porter's political and aesthetic theories were formed in the 1920s and 1930s during her experiences in Mexico and Europe, where art and politics combined in revolution and war. Her distaste for propagandistic art led to her own beliefs about art and the role of the artist in society. She saw art as one of two possibilities (the other was religion) for pointing people in the general direction of truth, but in her fiction she rarely depicts artists who succeed. There are bad poets such as Carlos in "Virgin Violeta," the journalist of "That Tree," and Uncle Gabriel of "Old Mortality"; shallow musicians in "Flowering Judas"; and misguided painters such as Rubén and his circle in "The Martyr." Good artists are represented by primitives, the young reed player in "Flowering Judas," Uncle Jimbilly in "The Witness," and the woodcarver in *Ship of Fools.* Charles Upton of "The Leaning Tower" is an apprentice artist, still being formed but potentially good if he remains sincere and avoids contrivance.

Although Porter held a belief in God and found beauty and power in some religious rituals, she was often critical of what she regarded as the abuses of institutional religion, which she said provided unsatisfactory answers to the most basic questions about life. At its worst it strengthens the malignity of ignorance. Herbert Klein recalls Porter's telling him that "we are groping around in the dark, like in a cellar, with only the feeble flame of our reason to aid us. And along comes the theologian and blows out the light."[12] Throughout her fiction there are more empty religious characters who merely go through the forms of religion than there are truly good religious characters. María Concepción's Catholicism is a facade that collapses under the weight of her primitivism; Laura's Catholicism has been discarded in favor of the religion of revolution; Granny Weatherall's Catholic faith has not provided satisfying answers for her, as it has not for Rosaleen O'Toole ("The Cracked Looking-Glass") or the characters in "A Day's Work"; the Protestant fundamentalism of the Thompsons ("Noon Wine") and the Whipples ("He") has offered no solutions to life's mysteries or solace for life's suffering; the Lutheranism of the Müllers in "Holiday" is surface only; and Herr Löwenthal is a discredit to his Judaism. Only Dr. Schumann of *Ship of Fools* is a completely religious man who is at peace with himself.

Porter's distrust of formulaic religion corresponds with her lack of faith in systems in general and political systems in particular. Illustrating her political themes are persons from opposite ends of the political spectrum, revolutionaries on the one hand who wish to change one system for another, and at the other extreme, the preservers of political order and tradition. Throughout her canon she expresses her cynicism by depicting characters like the repugnant Braggioni of "Flowering Judas," the played-out revolutionaries of "Hacienda"; the proponents of Nazism in "The Leaning Tower" and *Ship of Fools*; and the patriotic exploiters in "Pale Horse, Pale Rider." Not far from reliance on the form of a political system or a religion is fidelity to a code of middle-class manners. Many of Porter's characters are class conscious, concerned with appearance and worried about what their neighbors will think. Such superficial values motivate the Thompsons in "Noon Wine," Mrs. Whipple in "He," Lacey Halloran in "A Day's Work," and a variety of passengers on the *Vera*.

The great majority of Porter's central characters are women who together provide a commentary on the evolutionary role of women in the twentieth century, what Jane DeMouy calls "a sensitive prophecy for contemporary femininity."[13] Besides Porter's autobiographical protagonists who in varying degrees succeed in resolving inner conflicts, other women like María Concepción and Aunt Nannie ("The Fig Tree" and "The Witness") endure because they are as natural as the earth. If a woman tries to fulfill an idealized version of herself like Violeta in "Virgin Violeta" or Miranda in "Old Mortality," or to escape her femaleness like Laura in "Flowering Judas" or Mrs. Treadwell in *Ship of Fools*, she is inviting guilt and torment through a sense of self-betrayal. Women must be willing to assume, like Grandmother Sophie Jane Rhea Gay of "The Old Order" and Jenny Brown of *Ship of Fools*, what DeMouy calls the "burden of freedom."[14]

A group of characters who stand apart from the others are what Porter might have called the grotesques, those who seem to exist beyond realism or at least to take on symbolic overtones associated with the journey motif. They are often otherworldly, mysterious, sometimes mute or inarticulate, suggesting depths that link them to life's secrets. In folklore and romance, and even in the works of Henry James and Hawthorne, both of whom Porter admired, such characters are functional, serving to direct the protagonist toward truths or to signal the availability of truth, whether or not the protagonist is able to recognize it. These characters in Porter's fiction are Old Lupe in "María Concepción," He in "He," the clown and the dwarf in "The Circus," Helton in "Noon Wine," Ottilie in "Holiday," and Herr Glocken in *Ship of Fools*.

Porter's grand design and her secondary themes are dramatized by recurring characters and supported by her style. Her style has been described consistently as pure, simple, beautiful; it is also decidedly classical. She was the careful crafter of fiction, using the classical concept of the artist as "maker" to describe the work of the artist.[15] She often spoke of the James-minded people and the Whitman-minded people and declared that she, herself, was firmly on the side of James. M. M.

Liberman points out that in James, Porter obviously saw the triumph of "making," the effective ordering of experience by the means of style.[16]

Within the overall simplicity of her style and the evidence of careful craftsmanship, other classical elements are apparent. Immediately noticeable is Porter's plain vocabulary, which belies the complexity of her artistic vision. She once told an interviewer, "There is a basic pure human speech that exists in every language. And that is the language of the poet and the writer." She attacked "scientific language" and "the jargon of trades" and went on to explain:

You have to speak clearly and simply and purely in a language that a six-year-old child can understand; and yet have the meanings and the overtones of language, and the implications, that appeal to the highest intelligence—that is, the highest intelligence that one is able to reach. I'm not sure that I'm able to appeal to the highest intelligence, but I'm willing to try.[17]

The logical ordering of her syntax is also rooted in classical rhetoric. She favored compound and periodic sentences with coordinating conjunctions that led easily to Homeric rhythms and catalogues, which often appear in the form of parallel grammatical structures. Such an example occurs in a description of Juan in "María Concepción": "He was walking in the early sunshine, smelling the good smells of ripening cactus-figs, peaches, and melons, of pungent berries dangling from the pepper trees, and the smoke of his cigarette under his nose."[18] Robert B. Heilman identifies numerous examples of this stylistic trait in *Ship of Fools*.[19] Liberman cites in "Old Mortality" an excellent representative of Porter's periodic sentences, which, in his words, represent "in language . . . a world properly and permanently ordered."[20] The sentence reads:

During vacation on their grandmother's farm, Maria and Miranda, who read as naturally and constantly as ponies crop grass, and with much the same kind of pleasure, had by some happy chance laid hold of some forbidden reading matter, brought in and left there with missionary intent, no doubt, by some Protestant cousin. (193)

Liberman explains, "To the end of periodicity, 'forbidden reading matter' is brought in nearly at the conclusion, only ahead of 'missionary intent' and 'Protestant cousin.' "[21] With its delayed emphasis, the syntax sets up the tension in the story between opposing values within the Southern setting. Such syntax also reveals Porter's respect for the classical laws of unity and coherence.

Porter's classical rhetoric becomes an instrument of detachment, which also is achieved by one of her point-of-view techniques that is a form of stream of consciousness. Although Porter often presents dialogue and thoughts directly, equally often she presents dialogue and thoughts indirectly, without quotation marks, as if the statements or thoughts have been melted down in the author's consciousness, condensed, and shaped for the reader's apprehension. For example, all of "Rope" is presented in this form of distilled and detached dialogue. Whenever Porter uses the method, the irony in the work is amplified.

Porter's irony is sometimes simply verbal and at other times tragic and cosmic. She achieves structural irony in the Miranda stories, in which the simplicity of a younger Miranda's viewpoint is measured against the viewpoint of an older and wiser Miranda, and dramatic irony occurs when Miranda's naïveté contrasts with the greater knowledge of the reader. T. S. Eliot said that such a juxtaposition of viewpoints constituted within a work "an internal equilibrium" that was essential to irony.[22] I. A. Richards' similar concept of irony as a balance of opposites was developed by Robert Penn Warren, Cleanth Brooks, and others of Porter's twentieth-century contemporaries and friends into a theory that the greatest works incorporate the writer's own "ironic" awareness of opposite and complementary attitudes.[23] Warren describes Porter's irony as "irony with a center, never irony for its own sake. It simply implies," he says, "a refusal to accept the formula, the ready-made solution, the hand-me-down morality, the word for the spirit. It affirms, rather, the constant need for exercising discrimination, the arduous obligation of the intellect in the face of conflicting dogmas, the need for exercising as much of the human faculty as possible."[24]

OVERVIEW

Although irony creates subtle complexities within Porter's art, perhaps the greatest difficulty within her style has been her symbolism, which has generally presented readers with enigmas. Much critical controversy has surrounded the symbolic meaning of the dove, ring, and grave in "The Grave," the flowering judas tree in "Flowering Judas," the cracked looking-glass in "The Cracked Looking-Glass," the leaning tower in "The Leaning Tower," the rope in "Rope," the purse in "Theft," and the dreams in "María Concepción," "Flowering Judas," "Pale Horse, Pale Rider," "The Leaning Tower," and *Ship of Fools.* Porter, who told an interviewer, "I never consciously took or adopted a symbol in my life,"[25] on another occasion explained her understanding of symbolism in literature:

Symbolism happens of its own self and it comes out of something so deep in your own consciousness and your own experience that I don't think that most writers are at all conscious of their use of symbols. I never am until I see them. They come of themselves because they belong to me and have meaning to me, but they come of themselves. I have no way of explaining them. . . . And I suppose you don't invent symbolism."[26]

The importance Porter gave to symbols is often confirmed in the titles she chose for her stories. The dominant symbol is often in a story's title, as it is in "The Circus," "The Fig Tree," "The Grave," "Flowering Judas," "That Tree," "Rope," "Hacienda," "The Cracked Looking-Glass," and "The Leaning Tower." Light and dark images, which occur throughout her work, as one might expect in a canonical theme of the journey to awareness, also function symbolically.

Animals and birds are important in Porter's fiction, and although they may exist as living entities that take on symbolic meaning (such as the rabbit in "The Grave"), often they are presented only figuratively, usually in similes but sometimes in metaphors, serving as instruments of Porter's essentially humanistic philosophy. Her technique may have grown out of her familiarity with the Homeric simile, which often depended on a comparison with animal nature. She implies that animals offer to humans the opportunity for discerning an important truth. If humans can identify with animals and then perceive the difference between themselves and animals, they have understood the human soul and the meaning of human life. It is the most fundamental truth the young Miranda acquires, and it is the fundamental truth that many passengers on board the *Vera* in *Ship of Fools* miss.

Porter's style changed little over the years. The same pure language of "María Concepción" exists in *Ship of Fools*, as do the same grammatical structures and diction. If there is any difference, it is that the irony of the first story is intensified in the long novel. Porter's style is recognizably classical in its orderliness and clarity, but it is hers in the fusion of its classical elements to its intensity and its irony, with built-in paradoxes, which Warren described as its "tissue of contradictions."[27] Her style is a window to her people and themes, an "emanation," as Heilman says, "of the materials themselves."[28] She is a realist in the complete sense of both style and theme, in her careful attention to the details of verisimilitude, and in her insistence upon the pragmatic function of will within the boundaries of natural, universal laws. Those who would grasp Porter's meanings should recognize first the arduous quest for truth that underlies the canon and then the classical humanism that infuses her work. The style grows out of her worldview and is consistent with it.

Notes

1. Louise Bogan, "Flowering Judas," *New Republic* 64 (Oct. 1930): 277–78.

2. Yvor Winters, "Major Fiction," *Hound & Horn* 4 (Jan. 1931): 303–305.

3. John Chamberlain, "Books of the Times," *New York Times* 11 Oct. 1935: 23.

4. Lewis Gannett, "Books and Things," *New York Herald Tribune* 30 Mar. 1939: 23.

5. Paul Rosenfeld, "An Artist in Fiction," *Saturday Review of Literature* 19 (1 Apr. 1939): 7.

6. Robert Penn Warren, "Katherine Anne Porter: (Irony with a Center)," *Kenyon Review* 4 (1942): 29.

7. See John W. Aldridge, "Art and Passion in Katherine Anne Porter," *Time to Murder and Create: The Contemporary Novel in Crisis* (New York: David McKay, 1966): 178–84.

8. Edmund Wilson, "Katherine Anne Porter," *New Yorker* 20 (1944): 64–66. See also James William Johnson, "Another Look at Katherine Anne Porter," *The Virginia Quarterly Review* 36 (Autumn 1960): 598–613; and William L. Nance, *Katherine Anne Porter and the Art of Rejection* (Chapel Hill: University of North Carolina Press, 1964).

9. *The Collected Essays and Occasional Writings* (New York: Delacorte Press, 1970) 457.

10. Cited by Darlene Harbour Unrue, *Truth and Vision in Katherine Anne Porter's Fiction* (Athens: University of Georgia Press, 1985) 4.

11. Unrue 36.

12. Joan Givner, *Katherine Anne Porter: A Life* (New York: Simon and Schuster, 1982) 258.

13. Jane DeMouy, *Katherine Anne Porter's Women: The Eye of Her Fiction* (Austin: University of Texas Press, 1983) 15.

14. De Mouy 15.

15. Enrique Hank Lopez, "A Country and Some People I Love," *Harper's* Sept. 1965: 59–69.

16. M. M. Liberman, *Katherine Anne Porter's Fiction* (Detroit: Wayne State University Press, 1971) 52.

17. Barbara Thompson, "Katherine Anne Porter: An Interview," *Paris Review* No. 29 (1963): 108.

18. *The Collected Stories of Katherine Anne Porter* (New York: Harcourt, Brace and World, 1965) 12. Further references will be noted parenthetically.

19. See Robert B. Heilman, "*Ship of Fools:* Notes on Style," *Four Quarters* 12 (Nov. 1962): 46–55.

20. Liberman 44.

21. Liberman 44.

22. T. S. Eliot, "Andrew Marvell" (1921), *Selected Essays* (New York: Harcourt, Brace and World, 1960): 262.

23. See I. A. Richards, "The Imagination," *Principles of Literary Criticism* (New York: Harcourt, Brace and World, 1925): 247–50.

24. Warren 42.

25. Thompson 107.

OVERVIEW

26. "Recent Southern Fiction: A Panel Discussion," *Bulletin of Wesleyan College* 41 (Jan. 1961): 12.

27. Warren 42.

28. Heilman 55.

CHAPTER TWO

Mexico

Katherine Anne Porter went to Mexico in 1920 and, as she said, "ran smack into the Obregón Revolution," which provided her with "the most marvelous, natural, spontaneous experience" of her life.[1] That first visit lasted about a year. She returned in the spring of 1922 and left before the year was out; and she went back in 1930 and stayed until August 1931, when she left for Europe on the voyage that provided the inspiration for *Ship of Fools*. Although her time in Mexico between 1920 and 1931 constituted less than three years, there is no doubt that the events there during the 1920s shaped her career in important ways and that she formed most of her technical and philosophical theories during the decade.

Porter's first two visits provided the material for all of her Mexican stories except "Hacienda," and the last visit provided the perspective that is evident in "Hacienda." All the stories provide a commentary on the revolution Porter encountered. "María Concepción," "The

MEXICO

Martyr," "Virgin Violeta," and "Flowering Judas" treat the obstacles to the fulfillment of the revolution's aims; "Hacienda" is a study of the revolution's failure; and "That Tree" explores why expatriates were drawn to revolutionary Mexico in the 1920s. In addition to the subject of the revolution, the stories share common themes and stylistic traits. All the stories contain a general theme of betrayal and discovery of betrayal. The moment of disillusionment is a pivotal point in "María Concepción" and "Virgin Violeta"; partial disillusionment provides the conclusion to "Flowering Judas"; illusions are exploited by already disillusioned cynics in "Hacienda"; and a refusal to relinquish one's illusions is an important point in "The Martyr" and "That Tree." Sexual vitality is also a dominant theme. It is instinctual motivation in "María Concepción." It is repressed in "Virgin Violeta," "Flowering Judas," and "That Tree." It is perverted in "Hacienda," and it is diverted to idealism or materialism in "The Martyr."

The stories have the same surface style of all of Porter's works, but subtle differences are exhibited here, as Porter refined and tested narrative methods. Her experiments with viewpoint are dramatically apparent in "María Concepción," "Flowering Judas," the first version of "Hacienda," and the two versions of "That Tree." A comparison of "María Concepción" and "Flowering Judas" reveals the more elaborate use Porter developed for the dream vision, which in the early story is a simple proof of María Concepción's fulfillment of a thwarted maternalism but in "Flowering Judas" has be-

come a complex allegorical representation of the protagonist's deepest fears. Like all her works, the Mexican
stories were drawn from either Porter's own experience,
or someone else's that, as she said, became hers upon
hearing it.[2]

"María Concepción"

"María Concepción," published in *Century* magazine in 1922, was no exception. The story grew out of an
account given her by Professor William Niven, an aged
archaeologist, who had gone to Mexico in the last part
of the nineteenth century to excavate the ancient Mayan
and Aztec ruins around Mexico City and whom Porter
had met soon after her arrival in 1920. Niven, by her
own account, told her the story of his foreman Juan,
who was married to a woman named María but had
a teenage sweetheart as well. The literary interest of
the anecdote lay in the villagers' refusal to incriminate
María after she murdered the sweetheart and took the
girl's baby for her own.[3] By the time Porter reproduced
the story as fiction, adding minor characters, events,
and details, it had taken on larger symbolic and universal meanings. The story is also rich with the atmosphere of the early years of the artistic renaissance in
Mexico, a cultural and social movement that was an attempt to resurrect the ancient past of Mexico and bring
it into harmony with twentieth-century political aims.

MEXICO

"María Concepción" is a story in which primitive instinct proves stronger than social customs and learned behavior. María Concepción is an Indian woman who has accepted the conqueror's religion, but when the test comes, the savage ways prevail over the civilized religion's forms. Within that framework contradictions and paradoxes abound. María Concepción has no "faith," she says, in old Lupe's charms, but she cannot read the directions on bottles of medicine she buys instead of relying on Lupe's charred owls bones and rabbit entrails. The Indians dig for Givens, the outsider who values their past, while they themselves do not; Givens condescends to his Indian diggers, "for their primitive childish ways," but María Concepción condescends to Givens for his civilized distaste for killing fowl and for the fact that he has no woman to cook for him. Givens is patriarchal in the excavating society, and yet he lacks the strength to be a moral guide for his workers. His jokes about Juan's infidelities point ahead to a specific concern that emerges from time to time in Porter's canon and is most fully developed in *Ship of Fools*, in which she implies that patriarchy, in whatever form, is demeaning. George Hendrick remarks that from the outset in "María Concepción" Porter "introduces the reader to the ironic distance between things as they are and as they should be, between truth and fiction, between expectation and fulfillment, between art and life." He says that Porter "lays bare the ambiguities of life."[4]

The most important irony developed in the story is that even though twentieth-century man intellectually has rejected his primitive past, primitive instinct continues to reassert itself over civilized reason. Words and phrases like *unaccountably, involuntarily*, and *hardly knowing what he did* show that the primitive functions according to instinctual or mythological patterns. In this story there is a hint of the Adam and Eve and Lilith myth, which Porter represented in her poem "Measures for Song and Dance" (1950), and the myth of the scapegoat. Juan's sweetheart, María Rosa, becomes the scapegoat for all the villagers, who protect María Concepción in an ancient ritual and code of justice that defies the laws of the civilized government. The image of blindness, which was to serve Porter throughout her canon, is used here to suggest the unconscious, unreasoning forces that take over in the sequence of events after María Concepción is betrayed by Juan and María Rosa. María Concepción's face is "blind-looking" after Juan and María Rosa leave for the war, and after Juan saves María Concepción, he feels "a vast blind hurt."

Other images and symbols are plentiful in the story. Allen Tate observed that the story is written in primary colors, and indeed red, blue, and yellow appear throughout as images associated with the natural and the primitive.[5] Yellow is the color of honey, used universally as the symbol of earthly pleasures, and it is the color of the maguey leaves and María Concepción's eyes after she murders María Rosa; red is the color of the earth; and blue is more complex: it is the color of the far-off mountains (representing the faraway past), María Concepción's rebozo, the tassels on Juan's hat, and the

MEXICO

lining of María Rosa's coffin. It is finally primitive instinct (represented by primary colors) that kills María Rosa and protects María Concepción.

Another important symbol of primitivism is the cactus, which points to the destructive element within primitivism. It is this that María Concepción, as a "good Christian" woman, senses she must avoid. The first sentence in the story illustrates the symbolism: "María Concepción walked carefully, keeping to the middle of the white dusty road, where the maguey thorns and the treacherous curved spines of organ cactus had not gathered so profusely." The cactus is described a little later as being like bared knife blades, foreshadowing María Concepción's killing of María Rosa with a knife. After seeing Juan and María Rosa among the beehives, María Concepción burns all over, "as if a layer of tiny fig-cactus bristles, as cruel as spun glass, had crawled under her skin" (6). With all her careful attention she has not been able to avoid the "thorns," and it is from here on that she becomes murderous. Later, when she realizes that involuntarily she is on her way to kill María Rosa, she sits under a "sheltering thorny bush" and gives herself over to her long sorrow.

The thorns of the cactus are an implicit connection to the pattern of Christian imagery and symbolism in the story, linked of course to the crown of thorns, Christ's crucifixion, and betrayal. Other parts of the pattern include María Concepción's going to the church and "kneeling with her arms spread in the form of a cross" (9), Juan's celebrating in the "Death and Resurrection" pulque shop the birth of his and María Rosa's baby, María Concepción's crawling to Juan after the murder, as he had seen her crawl toward the shrine at Guadalupe Villa, Juan's instructing María Concepción in her line of defense as if he were instructing her in a catechism, their lighting candles by which to eat, Juan's flinging his arms "up and outward" after the dreadful ordeal with the gendarmes is over, and finally María Concepción's sitting with her head bowed over María Rosa's child, the posture of an idealized Madonna, "aware of a strange, wakeful happiness" (21). The Christian imagery and symbolism serve irony again; the surface image is Christian, but the deep reality is the force of primitive instinct.

María Concepción's dream is the first of many dreams in Porter's fiction, which present the dreamer with some form of truth. María Concepción dreams that the child is hers, and she is "resting deliciously." The child is hers now by a law as old as the ancient civilizations of Mexico, and her delicious resting is the happiness that comes from the settling of a wrong according to an ancient code of justice.

"The Martyr"

In "María Concepción" Porter is subtly illustrating one of the difficulties the leaders of Mexico faced in trying to educate the Indian. In "The Martyr," her second original story (*Century*, 1923), she is illustrating another obstacle to the fulfillment of the revolution's aims. She herself was caught up in the events of the Mexican revolution when she first arrived there in 1920. Her letters to her family and friends reveal an idealistic fervor as she describes carrying secret messages, teaching dancing in one of the socialist schools, and consorting with archaeologists, artists, government officials, and bandits. When Porter was planning, "María Concepción," she wrote in an essay about the Mexican revolution that the revolution had not touched the hearts of the Mexican people, and she lamented that there was not the commitment by writers to the Mexican revolution that there had been to the 1917 Russian Revolution. Porter charged that Mexican writers were concerned with nothing more important than "the pain of unrequited love."[6] When she returned to Mexico in 1922, she witnessed the triumphant reentry into Mexico of the painter Diego Rivera, who was responsible for providing the revolutionary spark that the writers had failed to offer. For the remainder of 1922 Porter observed the brilliant murals that the revolution produced, usually under the direction or inspiration of Diego, but she became disillusioned with Diego's self-aggrandizement and the adulation paid him by his admirers. "The Martyr" is about Diego and his first wife, Guadalupe Marin; it is about the charade of unrequited love she saw as pervasive in the paternalistic Mexican society;

and it is about the replacement of love with a shallow substitute.

The ironic tone prevails. The narrative voice has become more intensely ironic than it was in "María Concepción," and the distance between the ideal and the actual is apparent from the outset. The callous, bored, materialistic Isabel, who calls people by the names of animals (the obese Rubén is "Churro," a pet name for small dogs as well as for sweet cakes; the people who come to pay homage to Rubén are called "sheep"), is far from the Isabel Rubén memorializes as "angelic" with "pretty little tricks and ways." There is bitter irony in the portrayal of the Mexican artists, Rubén's friends, who remember Isabel as the "lean she-devil" but nevertheless propagate the lie. After Rubén dies, they memorialize him as a "martyr to love" (37) even though it is abundantly clear that he eats himself to death.

The largest irony in this story is contained in its symbolism, which is damaging because it is too personal to Diego and too particular to support the more important theme of displaced love. Before Isabel leaves, Rubén is beginning the nineteenth drawing of her, and according to Isabel's farewell note, there were to be twenty. She says that she is going away with "someone who . . . will make a mural with fifty figures of me in it, instead of only twenty" (34). The meaning of the number symbolism is elusive without the knowledge that one of Diego's murals, which Porter had seen, had twenty female figures in it. It was entitled "Creation" and portrayed, in addition to Woman as counterpart to

Man, personified ideals: Knowledge, Fable, Erotic Poetry, Tradition, Tragedy, Prudence, Justice, Strength, Continence, Science, Dance, Music, Song, Comedy, Charity, Hope, Faith, and Wisdom. The nineteenth female figure, Wisdom, is the most important, according to Diego's notes of explanation for the mural. The twentieth figure is the Tree, symbol of female fertility.[7]

"The Martyr" remains more important as a step in Porter's developing technique and philosophy than it does as a successful story in its own right. Like "María Concepción" it contains a religious structure (Rubén "adores" Isabel and dies a martyr, even if to gluttony) that serves as a reminder of the distance of the ideal from the story's events. It is built around an ironic center; and it grew out of Porter's personal experience. The simple language is present, and the preference for periodic sentences with antithesis and balance to underscore the ever-present irony, is more apparent.

"Virgin Violeta"

"Virgin Violeta" was published in *Century* in 1924, and it, too, grew out of events in the Mexican cultural renaissance, although it anticipates some of the themes to be developed later in the Miranda cycle. In some respects it continues the theme of idealized love that is presented in "The Martyr." In this story, however, the conflict is centered within a single character, the adolescent Violeta, and the opposition to idealized love is sensual love, another version of the disparity between truth and appearance.

According to Givner, the kernel of the story was presented to Porter during her first visit to Mexico City in 1920–21, when she met the Nicaraguan poet Salomón de la Selva, who told her a disgusting story of a mean and deliberate seduction of a young girl.[8] As with her other stories, the artistic rendering of the experience changed it in important ways. For the story she drew upon her knowledge of the aristocratic Spanish upper class. While the ironic conflict between the idealized and the sensual remains the most important theme of the story, she presents as secondary themes the disservice of the Catholic Church in fostering an unrealistic view of love, a subject Porter took up in several essays, and the paternalism of the Church and the Mexican society that promotes sexism, a feminist theme much a part of the cultural revolution and one she hinted at in "María Concepción." In "Virgin Violeta" also is an enlargement of animal imagery present in "The Martyr."

Violeta, who is a prototype of Miranda and of several characters in *Ship of Fools*, (as Blanca is the prototype of Miranda's older sister Maria in "The Old Order" and "Old Mortality"), is nearly fifteen years old and enjoying a romantic, idealized view of love, encouraged by the Church's adulation of the Virgin and fostered by Violeta's reading of her cousin Carlos' sentimental love poems. Violeta imagines a perfect future, a perpetual festival, in which she would be a virgin princess adored

by fascinating young men and most of all by Carlos.
There is no place for carnality in Violeta's dream, and
when she sees hints of it, such as the moisture on Carlos' underlip, she is disturbed without knowing why
(23). She is also disturbed by the sensual playfulness
between Blanca and Carlos. Violeta's ideal is visualized
in the painting "Pious Interview between the Most Holy
Virgin Queen of Heaven and Her Faithful Servant St.
Ignatius Loyola," in which the saint grovels before the
Virgin in a wooden posture of ecstasy.

The conflict within Violeta is between her idealized
view of love and her own awakening sensuality, which
she represses. She is confused because she cannot understand "why things that happen outside of people
were so different from what she felt inside of her."
Moreover, the "something inside her" feels as if it is
"enclosed in a cage too small for it," and it is the Church
which is the "terrible, huge cage" that seems "too
small" (26). When Carlos steals a kiss in the sunroom,
Violeta is "sharply hurt, as if she had collided with a
chair in the dark" and becomes sick as she always does
when she is "called up to explain things to Mother Superior." When Carlos leaves the family gathering and
starts to give Violeta a perfunctory goodbye kiss, she
screams uncontrollably. Because she cannot "settle the
questions brooding in her mind," Violeta, like her literary descendant Miranda in "Old Mortality," rejects both
the ideal and the real. She makes ugly caricatures of
Carlos and leaves the convent, declaring there is "nothing to be learned there."

Porter's use of animal imagery is related to her belief that if one cannot see both similarity to and difference from animals, then a painful unhappiness or utter confusion will result. Violeta's identification of Carlos with cats (he has "furry golden eyebrows") and birds of prey (he is like a macaw) points out her sensing the animal appeal of Carlos and also the danger he is to her romantic ideal. Violeta herself is described in animal images; Carlos tells her she is young "like a little newborn calf"; she has "the silence and watchfulness of a young wild animal, but no native wisdom"; and after her final hysteria, she whimpers "like a puppy" (32). But Violeta cannot recognize her animal nature, even when she sees herself before the "loathsome" Carlos, "almost as if his face were a mirror" (29), an image Porter will use later. The recognition must be denied, the awakening sensuality repressed and the ideal rejected. The ironic voice vibrates with thematic paradoxes.

"Flowering Judas"

Porter did not include "The Martyr" or "Virgin Violeta" in her first collection of stories. She told a student that she had omitted them because she had not been satisfied with them once she saw them in print.[9] A story which did satisfy her was "Flowering Judas," one of her best-known and most often anthologized stories. Although she took notes for the story in 1921, she did

MEXICO

not complete it until 1929, the year before her last sustained visit to Mexico.[10] She described the writing of "Flowering Judas" in Whit Burnett's *This Is My Best*. It developed from the state of revolutionary affairs in Mexico in 1920 and a memory of an experience with her friend Mary Doherty, who became the real-life counterpart of Laura, even though Porter included something of herself in the character as well.

When Porter took notes for the story in 1921 she still had some idealistic faith in the revolution, but by the time she wrote the story she had become disillusioned, and this cynicism is evident in the story's tone. The first paragraph describes Braggioni in repugnant images. At the end of the paragraph, the maid greets the returning Laura at the door saying "with a flicker of a glance towards the upper room 'He Waits.' " The allusion to Christ and the Last Supper (Mark 14: 12–16) establishes at once the central paradox of religion vs. revolution and anticipates the theme of betrayal. It is already clear that this representative of the revolution, Braggioni, is particularly unworthy of the comparison. As the story unfolds, the conflict is amplified. The revolutionary ideal has replaced Laura's discarded faith, her childhood Catholicism, but Laura has not settled everything because "she cannot help feeling that she has been betrayed irreparably by the disunion between her way of living and her feeling of what life should be" (91).

Betrayal is the dominant theme of this story. Laura feels betrayed by the revolution that did not fulfill the early idealistic aims of the movement. Braggioni, who was a poet in those early days, can sing now only of unrequited love, as does the shock-haired youth, who sings in Laura's patio. Laura also betrays the revolution's ideal by stepping into a church to pray, knowing that discovery will cause a scandal, and by rejecting the machine, which is sacred to the movement (her private heresy is that she refuses to wear lace made on machines). If she feels betrayed by the Church that promised something Laura has not found, she also betrays her religion, which promises spiritual life, by replacing it with the revolution that practices death.

It is too simplistic to say that Laura betrays Eugenio by providing the drugs that make his suicide possible, but she does betray herself, and in a way that includes her responsibility to Eugenio. Laura has rejected her femininity, her maternalism, her nurturing nature. She has done so partly in unconscious self-protection because she knows that only as long as she is a virgin will she be safe among Braggioni and others, who honor the ideal of chastity in their inherited chivalric code. But unconscious or not, the defense constitutes a rejection. Laura has managed the rejection by denying everything and encasing herself in a set of principles rather than facing reality ("she is not at home in the world"). By denying everything, by negating "all external events," she must also deny herself love. Every day she teaches children she does not love; they remain strangers to her, even though "she loves their tender round hands and their charming opportunist savagery" (97). As a courier for the revolutionists, she is required to knock on the door of strangers, kinship with whom she rejects with a "No. No. No." She is gradually perfecting herself "in the stoicism she strives to cultivate" (97).

The theme of betrayal is focused in the primary symbol in the story, the flowering Judas trees, which was inspired by T. S. Eliot's poem "Gerontion."[11] According to legend, Judas hanged himself from a redbud tree, and Eliot's poem names the tree "flowering judas." The symbolism of the Judas tree is completed in the dream when Laura eats the "bleeding" flowers as a ritual of Christian communion, but when she discovers they are Eugenio's body and blood, not Christ's, she awakes "trembling" and "afraid to sleep." What she thought was an act of contrition proves to be an act of destruction. Porter's use of the dream in this story is developing into a means by which her characters confront elemental truths.

Flowers are symbols in the story, and Porter identifies flowers with the female principle in her essay "Flower of Flowers" (1950) and in an unpublished sketch she wrote in the twenties about Xochitl, an ancient Mayan goddess, whose name means "flower."[12] The children whom Laura teaches "make her desk a fresh garden of flowers everyday," and when they write "We lov ar ticher" on the chalkboard, they draw "wreaths of flowers around the words" (95). Also she throws flowers (that symbolically wither) to the youth who serenades her. Other important symbolism in the story is that of machinery and oil, which Porter thought of as anti-life and opposite to flowers. Laura's fear and abhorrence of machines (identified with the revolution that was to free the peon from bondage) is linked to Braggioni, described as "oily" and "suety." Braggioni also is associated with animal imagery in the story. His voice is "furry," he has "yellow cat's eyes," and he "squeels" his songs.

Laura's partial awakening has been the result of a spiritual journey, symbolized by her walking through the streets of Mexico City. References in the story to the Sixteenth of September Street, the Merced Market, the Zócolo, Francisco I. Madero Avenue, the Paseo de la Reforma, Chapultepec Park (all names that have significance in the honorable history of Mexico's revolutions) provide a backdrop that has given momentary legitimacy to present revolutionary activity but also create a contrast between past honor and present corruption. Another journey, to death, which Eugenio offers her in her dream at the story's end, she chooses not to take. It remains for Miranda to make that journey in "Pale Horse, Pale Rider" and thus to complete the rite of passage that Laura barely begins.

"Hacienda"

Laura subconsciously awakened to the revolution's impending death, which already has occurred at the beginning of "Hacienda." "Hacienda" was published in a short form in 1932 in the *Virginia Quarterly Review*, and an expanded version appeared as a book in 1934. The latter version is a more analytical representation of the events which inspired the first version. In July 1931 some of Porter's friends had arranged for her to visit the Hacienda Tetlapajac where the renowned Russian director Sergei Eisenstein was filming what would be called *Que Viva Mexico.* Because most of the characters in "Hacienda" are fictional counterparts of the real people present during Porter's visit (Eisenstein; his collaborator, Gregori Alexandrov; his Swedish-born cameraman, Eduard Tissé; the hacienda owner, don Julio Saldívar, and his wife; the business manager, Hunter Kimbrough; and the art director, Adolfo Best-Maugard), the story was taken to be almost a documentary. When Porter published the expanded version, wanting readers to focus on the artistic themes of the story, she attached a disclaiming note that "all characters and situations in this story are entirely fictional and do not portray an actual person."

"Hacienda" is Porter's most bitter comment on the Mexican revolution. Each of the previous Mexican stories represented Porter's views on the cultural revolution at a particular point in its unfolding, but "Hacienda" is the depiction of the aftermath of what Porter considered the failed revolution. The detachment of the first-person narrator is the result of her despair and resignation. The story is made up of several plots: the background story of the making of the film; the triangle of don Genaro, his wife, doña Julia, and her lover Lolita; and the story of Justino's killing his sister Rosalita.

All the plots intertwine and develop the same large theme of appearance versus reality. The filmmaking is the perfect frame for the other plots, dealing as it does with the creating of illusion.

Within the appearance-versus-reality theme are woven other themes. As Robert Perry has pointed out, the theme of change is pervasive.[13] The Indians have been promised change, and now they can ride on trains instead of burros. But their quality of living and their relationship to the power structure have not changed at all. Andreyev, one of the filmmakers, explains ironically to the narrator during the opening train ride that the object of the film is to show that the earlier plight of the Indian has been swept away by the revolution. The most common form of change at the hacienda is death, represented by the pervasive smell of the decaying maguey used in the making of pulque. The traditional values of the past aristocracy have changed for the worse, as the grandfather's degradation illustrates; traditional roles of husbands and wives have changed, and, moreover, traditional roles of men and women have changed. Doña Julia is childlike, plays with dolls, dresses in Chinese dress or Hollywood costume, and develops a lesbian relationship with her husband's mistress. Don Genaro does not rule his hacienda; he rushes back and forth between the capital and the hacienda, "always at top speed," says art director Betancourt, "and never on time anywhere" (154). In place of traditional values of the past, there is weakness and perversion, not admirable substitutes for what is lost, and the blind force of unconscious savagery has asserted itself without the restraints of the aristocratic structure. The Indian boy Justino's killing of his sister Rosalita hints paradoxically at both incestuous and homosexual motives. Andreyev says, "Imagine a man's friend betraying him so, and with a woman, and a sister! He was furious. He did not know what he was doing, maybe" (167). Porter also explores what in "St. Augustine and the Bullfight" (1955) she called the bloodlust, the enjoyment of death and the instinctual attraction humans have to it. The Indians' eyes dance with pleasure in retelling the story, and Kennerly, the film's American backer and Porter's representative Puritan, "licked his chops."

The symbols in "Hacienda" are obvious. Aside from the filmmaking, symbolizing the creation of illusion, what, in fact, the revolution has done, the making of pulque is a symbol of the decay of the revolution. The smell of the fermenting maguey is pervasive, like rotting milk and blood. The hacienda itself, a pulqueria, with all its surface evidence of the changing of orders, continues to exist by a feudal system that depends on an ancient process. The "modern" hacienda, a symbol of Mexico, continues to survive only by exploitation of the Indian, an abuse which the revolution promised to abolish. Machines symbolize the revolution, and they are valued particularly by don Genaro. A train ride opens the story, in the revised version, and automobiles, trains, and airplanes are discussed throughout; at the end of the story, the guests all depart by these means. The journeys that frame the story are ironic reminders that there has been no progress.

"That Tree"

"Hacienda" was Porter's last comment on the revolution, but it was not her last story set in Mexico. "That Tree," published in the *Virginia Quarterly Review* in 1934, was inspired by the drama of the personal lives of Carlton Beals, an American journalist, and his wife Lillian, whom Porter knew in the early 1920s in Mexico.[14] While there are references in the story to the revolution—it is in the far background—the story is essentially about the Anglo-American expatriate community in Mexico. "That Tree" still lies with the frame of Porter's design. It is about appearance and reality and self-deception as people avoid available truth and seek idealistic lives that are forever out of reach. On a more immediate level Porter examines reasons people in the expatriate community were attracted to Mexico. THe unnamed journalist "had really wanted to be a cheerful bum lying under a tree in a good climate, writing poetry" (66). Before Miriam became his wife she wrote him about "how she longed to live in a beautiful dangerous place among interesting people who painted and wrote poetry, and how his letters came into her stuffy little world like a breath of free mountain air" (73–74). The journalist remembers "a gang of Americans like himself who were living a free life and studying the native customs" (78). Porter remarked in an essay she had written on D. H. Lawrence that "he had come to Mexico hoping to find in primitive people a center and a meaning to life."[15] The journalist and his wife seem to have less noble motives. It turns out, however, that the ideal of carefree living, symbolized by the tree, associated universally with knowledge, is irreconcilable with the indigenous American Puritan ethic. Miriam's Biblical name, her preference for Milton's poetry over her husband's, her school teaching, her primness, and her sexual repression represent her provinciality and her inability to accept the dark truths about human nature. But it is her judgment of the journalist that causes him to abandon his carefree life and work to become a successful journalist. And it is his success that brings Miriam back to Mexico. Thus, the illusion for both of them begins anew, and the conflict remains unsettled. It is the conflict within the American consciousness itself, between escape and responsibility, or perhaps between the frontier and civilization.

"That Tree" offers an especially interesting study of Porter's development of style. She revised the story before it appeared in the 1935 edition of *Flowering Judas and Other Stories*, and the change in point of view is noteworthy. In the first version, the story is told by a narrator who is present at the journalist's monologue and participates in the rendition by translating that monologue into an indirect description of his words, using direct quotations only when the journalist quotes someone else or when a conversation between the journalist and nearby patrons of the bar interrupts the flow of the journalist's musings. The narrator confirms her presence when she says, "He wondered if any of us had ever thought how impossible it is to explain or make other people see the special qualities in the person you love" and again when she says, "Both of us jumped nervously at an explosion in the street, the backfire of an automobile."[16] In the revised version, the first-person viewpoint is abandoned, but Porter implies the presence of a companion in the statement "They both jumped nervously at an explosion in the street, the backfire of an automobile" (68). Such a companion seems to be confirmed when the journalist says "to his guest," "For God's sake . . . let's have another drink" (74) and later when he observes, "Our glasses are empty again" (78). The guest/companion/auditor is mentioned explicitly near the end of the story: "His guest wished to say, 'Don't forget to invite me to your wedding,' but thought better of it" (79). With the changes in the revision Porter refines the story in several important ways. She moved the emphasis upon the ironic turn of events to an emphasis upon the psychological state of the journalist, who seems to be addressing himself rather than another person. Porter calls the nebulous companion only "the guest," but the journalist thinks of the companion as "the shadow opposite" and finally as a "mirror." The final version is both more complex and more realistic. Except for faint allusions in

MEXICO

"Old Mortality" and "The Leaning Tower" Porter left Mexico behind in "That Tree," using it again only as the opening scene of *Ship of Fools*, the place of embarkation for the *Vera*, just as it was the place of embarkation for her serious writing.

Notes

1. Barbara Thompson, "Katherine Anne Porter: An Interview," *Paris Review* No. 29 (1963): 97.

2. Thompson 103.

3. Hank Lopez, *Conversations with Katherine Anne Porter: Refugee from Indian Creek* (Boston and Toronto: Little, Brown, 1981) 69–72.

4. George Hendrick, *Katherine Anne Porter* (New York: Twayne, 1965) 30.

5. See Allen Tate, "A New Star," *Nation* 131 (October 1930); 352–53.

6. See *The Collected Essays* 401.

7. Bertram Wolfe, *The Fabulous Life of Diego Rivera* (New York: Stein and Day, 1963) 134–38.

8. Joan Givner, *Katherine Anne Porter: A Life* (New York: Simon and Schuster, 1982) 171–72.

9. Cited by Darlene Harbour Unrue, *Truth and Vision in Katherine Anne Porter's Fiction* (Athens: University of Georgia Press, 1985) 236, n. 22.

10. Unrue 80–81.

11. See Ray B. West, *Katherine Anne Porter* (Minneapolis: University of Minnesota Press, 1963) 10–11.

12. See Thomas F. Walsh, "Xochitl: Katherine Anne Porter's Changing Goddess," *American Literature* 52 (May 1980): 183–93.

13. Robert L. Perry, "Porter's 'Hacienda' and the Theme of Change," *Midwest Quarterly* 6 (Summer 1965): 403–15.

14. Unrue 133–35.
15. See "Quetzalcoatl," *The Collected Essays* 421.
16. "That Tree," *Virginia Quarterly Review* 10 (July 1934): 352–53.

CHAPTER THREE

The Old South

Porter's stories set in the South concern the Old Order and the New. The Old Order was a structured antebellum society that cherished aesthetic ideals at the same time it nurtured inequities indigenous to feudalism. In their feudal structure the Old Order aristocrats enjoyed privilege and comfort by encasing themselves in a detachment that ignored the bond of humanity and the cost in suffering that luxury exacted. Old Order descendants preserve the past by legend and fragile truths, to which reason and science are anathema. They often are in conflict with the New Order, made up of persons who consciously reject the romantic values and traditions of the past and of poor whites struggling to enter middle-class respectability. Porter explores this conflict in "The Old Order" and "Old Mortality," and in "Magic" she presents the effects of the aristocratic detachment.

"Magic"

"Magic" was written in 1927, while Porter was living in Salem, Massachusetts, working on her biography of Cotton Mather, which was never completed. "Magic" was published in 1928 in *transition*. According to Givner, it was based on a tale Porter had heard from a black maid who had worked on Basin Street in New Orleans.[1] The three-page story is an indirect dramatic monologue packed with irony and social, as well as philosophical, commentary. Written in a Jamesian style, in which the story's meaning is conveyed through implications, "Magic" is not an exploration of the supernatural that was said to have brought the girl Ninette back to the brothel. It rather explores social evil that evolves in inhumane class systems. The monologue is delivered by a maid who is dressing her employer's hair. It is interrupted only twice and then by directly quoted remarks by the employer, Madame Blanchard: "You are pulling a little here . . . and then what?" (4) and "Yes, and then?" (41)—questions asked in indifference that illustrate the story's theme of the assistance of evil by passive consent.

The New Orleans setting is well suited to the story's themes, with its mixture of castes and the practice of voodoo common among some of its inhabitants. During the time she was writing the story, Porter would have been reflecting upon evil, both moral and social, steeped as she was in those days not only with Cotton Mather and the Puritan notions of absolute evil but also with Hawthorne's brooding presence in Salem, where she was inspired to re-read all his works.[2] In addition, she had been actively involved the preceding year in protests in Boston against the handling of the Sacco-Vanzetti case and was taking notes about social injustice and the moral evil implicit in it, opinions that finally appeared in her long essay "The Never-Ending Wrong" (1977).

Ironies in "Magic" center on the disparity between what the maid says and what she means, which is ambiguous; on Madame Blanchard's surface purity (her name means white) and her inner impurity (she assists evil by her apathy); and on the dramatic parallel between Madame Blanchard with her Creole maid and the brothel's madam with the prostitute Ninette. As Hendrick points out, only an *e* separates Madame Blanchard from the madam of the fancy house, and the Creole maid establishes her relationship to Ninette by telling Madame Blanchard that she is "happy to be here" and recalling at the end of the story when Ninette returned to the brothel that she likewise was "happy to be there."[3]

The maid flatters Madame Blanchard ("Maybe you don't know what is a fancy house") and is solicitous of her comfort, saying she will tell the story to "rest" Madame while she brushes her hair. The seamy little story could rest Madame Blanchard only if it reinforced her smug remove from the sordid world it recreates; the story actually undermines the institutions of middle and upper class life that allow the Ninettes to suffer by an apathetic indulgence of social evil that does not invade the privileged stratum. There are subtle psychological probings here and bitter social commentary about class systems, slavery, and a loveless, corrupt society, commentary Porter makes also in "Hacienda."

"The Old Order"

In its vignette of the privileged class, "Magic" leads readily to an account of Miranda's coming to terms with the vestiges of old order values in her own family. "The Old Order," which includes the earliest and latest stages of Miranda's initiation, is a collection of seven short pieces published between 1935 and 1960. Porter first published "Two Plantation Portraits: The Witness and The Last Leaf" in the *Virginia Quarterly Review* in 1935. In the same year she published "The Grave" (*Virginia Quarterly Review*) and "The Circus" (*Southern Review*). In 1936 she published "The Old Order" in the *Southern Review*, but she renamed it "The Journey" in *The Collected Stories*, having already chosen "The Old Order" for the collective title of six of the pieces. "The Source," which is the introductory story in the series, was first published in *Accent* in 1941.

Porter did not begin putting the stories together until 1955, when the first six were included in a collection called *The Old Order: Stories of the South* (with "The Jilt-

THE OLD SOUTH

ing of Granny Weatherall," "He," "Magic," and "Old Mortality"). It was at this point that Porter arranged them in an order different from their chronological publication. She inserted "The Circus" between "The Witness" and "The Last Leaf," no doubt to show that Miranda's story was incorporated in the stories of the older generation. When "The Fig Tree," having been published in 1960 in *Harper's Magazine*, was added to the group in 1965 in *The Collected Stories*, it was placed after "The Last Leaf" but appropriately before "The Grave," which contains the last revelation of all the Miranda stories. The stories ostensibly are set in the Southwest after the family moved from Kentucky to eastern Texas near the Arkansas border, a region settled by slave owners from both the upper and lower South and suffused with feudal customs and values that are distinct from the freewheeling traditions of the old West.[4] In their retrospective segments, the stories depict the changing of orders and the post-bellum Southern economy that precipitated the family's move from the upper South to Texas.

The first two stories of "The Old Order," "The Source" and "The Journey," are told primarily in retrospect. "The Source" begins with the statement, "Once a year, in early summer, after school was closed and the children were to be sent to the farm, the Grandmother began to long for the country" (321), a declaration that depends for its authority upon the cumulative weight of the passage of years. The story unfolds indirectly, with only five statements in direct quotation: Grandmother's ritualistic justification for the annual summer trip to the farm ("I begin to feel the need of a little change and relaxation, too" [321]); her warning to her grown up son, who resists the inconveniences the move always brings ("Now Harry, now Harry!" [321]), which shows Grandmother's unshaken position of rule in the family; the Negro Hinry's greeting to Grandmother ("Howdy-do, Miss Sophia Jane!" [322]); and Grandmother's regular assessment of the condition of her favorite horse, Fiddler (typically "He's getting stiff in the knees" or "He's pretty short-winded this year" [325]), descriptions which she fails to see are true of her as well. "The Source" is the grandmother's story. Her past is summarized in references to the Civil War, to her widowhood, to her having planted orchards in three states, and to Aunt Nannie and the other Negroes on the farm who had been slaves. But it is also the beginning of Miranda's story. By calling Sophia Jane "the grandmother," Porter implies a child's perspective from which the events are seen. The grandmother's dignity and formidable efficiency are described as parts of her overall orderliness and her fondness for ritual. She is both the source of the family and the source of many of Miranda's views and strengths.

"The Journey" expands on the grandmother's past briefly outlined in "The Source." This second story begins in the later years of Grandmother and Aunt Nannie but shifts into retrospection to provide an account of their Kentucky past. The vehicle for the recounting of

THE OLD SOUTH

Sophia Jane's and Nannie's past is their reminiscences, in which they recreate their histories by selective recall and artistic shaping. Memory is the means by which they create order in the universe. They convince themselves that changes are aberrations and that "a series of changes might bring them, blessedly, back full-circle to the old ways they had known" (327). In this story Miranda, Maria, and Paul are named, showing their emerging importance, and an important philosophical point is subtly made which links Porter's technical use of animals and animal imagery to a specific social and moral position. Sophia Jane, the grandmother, chose the child Nannie, whom she called a "monkey," for her playmate the same day she received the pony "Fiddler." She did not know which she loved more. Her identifying the Negro child Nannie with animals is precisely what society has done in the buying and selling of slaves. Even when Nannie went to the big house to live with Sophia Jane, the kindness shown her was "not so indulgent, maybe, as that given to the puppies" (332).

Sophia Jane's courtship by and wedding to her second cousin Stephen Gay are briefly described as are the years of birthing and rearing children, her husband's death, the moves to Louisiana and Texas, and the marriages of her children. The story ends abruptly with the sudden death of the grandmother. Interspersed in the narrative are the grandmother's philosophical ideas that are in fact contradictory and account for the often paradoxical views held by Miranda. She disapproves of the

modern ways of her youngest son's wife, who represents the "new" woman, "who was beginning to run
wild, asking for the vote, leaving her home and going
out in the world to earn her own living . . . " (333); but
when Sophia Jane had been a young mother she had
flouted tradition by taking the ill Nannie's child to
nurse, horrifying both her husband and mother. And
even though she had had traditional aristocratic ideas
about a woman's place and responsibilities, when she
was widowed, she learned to do men's work and con-
duct men's business, accumulating enough wealth to
give each of her children land and money as wedding
gifts. Her contempt for men is traced, as are her indulgence of her grandchildren and her strength of
character.

In "The Source" the relationship between whites
and blacks in the South is observed. In "The Journey" it
is examined closely in the bond between Sophia Jane
and Nannie. Porter moves in still closer to study Uncle
Jimbilly, Nannie's husband, and Nannie herself in "The
Witness" and "The Last Leaf." "The Witness" reveals
Uncle Jimbilly's relationship to the three grandchildren
as he tells them horrible stories about slavery. "The Last
Leaf" describes Aunt Nannie's retreat into a little cabin
across the creek, a move that represents a retreat into
her pre-slavery past, an "aged Bantu woman of independent means, sitting on the steps, breathing the free
air" (349). She refuses to work for the family and
refuses to let her husband, Uncle Jimbilly, move in with

her, saying, "I don' aim to pass my las' days waitin on no man. . . . I've served my time, I've done my do, and dat's all" (351). These two stories illustrate change, both natural and social.

Throughout the first three stories Miranda's importance has emerged as she is traced from an unnamed grandchild to a more fully identified character. "The Circus," the first story in the series specifically about Miranda, focuses on the first stage of Miranda's initiation. It begins with a description of many members of the Gay family, some visiting from Kentucky, sitting on planks at the circus. The viewpoint, although omniscient, is restricted to Miranda, and the story unfolds from the little girl's perspective. It tells of the frightening experience of her first circus. The explosion of sound, color, and smell is overwhelming to Miranda, who is confronted with sordid facts of a world she is not ready to understand—the salacious looks of little boys, the crowd's bloodlust, their roaring with savage delight at the dangers endured by the tightrope walker, the cruel mouth and bone-white skull of the clown, and the dwarf's terrible grimace. She knows only that she is terribly afraid without knowing what she has seen: the human capacity for cruelty, lust without love, and death itself.

Charles Kaplan has made some important points about "The Circus," seeing it logically as one of the epiphanies in Miranda's growth to maturity, an epiphany that is a paradoxical vision of evil revealed at the heart of gaiety.[5] Animals and animal imagery serve to make the ironic point that is the core of the story's meaning. At the circus the audience is crowded together "lak fleas on a dog's ear"; Cousin Miranda Gay has wild gray eyes "like a colt's" (343); the little boys under the stands are "monkeys"; when the clown performs, his leg waves "like a feeler above his head," which he turns "like a seal from side to side"; and the dwarf at the entrance has eyes "like a near-sighted dog" (345). Miranda feels removed from all these "creatures" until the dwarf looks at her with "remote displeasure," which she identifies as a human look. It is a bridge to an important truth, and Miranda crosses it only subconsciously.

Porter continues to blur the boundaries between humans and animals as she shows the other returning children as having seen the animals at the circus in human terms. There were "darling little monkeys" in human dress who rode the ponies; trained goats that danced; and "a baby elephant that crossed his front feet and leaned against his cage and opened his mouth to be fed, *such* a baby!" This latter, pleasant, view of the relationship between animals and humans is a fantasy created by humans, Porter implies, because it gives way to Miranda's real, horrifying, view of the truth revealed in a dream state. Kaplan says that if the realist is "defined as one who resists self-deception, the realist in Miranda has been born as a result of this experience."[6]

"The Fig Tree" begins where "The Circus" ends in Miranda's developing awareness, an early point in the

THE OLD SOUTH

stage between innocence and experience. The story was begun in the 1920s and written in something close to its present form in the early 1930s, when Porter was planning and writing most of the other Miranda stories. The story begins with Aunt Nannie's dressing Miranda and, in the role of protector of the values and styles of her former oppressors, making sure Miranda's face is shaded with a bonnet lest she get freckles. The occasion is a journey, symbolic of life in that Miranda does not know the destination. Porter writes that Miranda "could never find out about anything until the last minute" and that she "was always being surprised" (352). The family in fact is going to Cedar Grove, which Miranda's father, Harry, calls Halifax, his word for Hell. The individual responses to Cedar Grove define the relativity of truth. Harry thinks of it as Hell because it is unpleasantly hot. Grandmother loves it because she has been going there for fifty summers, her feeling an indication of her affinity to both the past and tradition. Miranda thinks of it as idyllic, filled with images of watermelon, grasshoppers, Chinaberry trees, and sleeping hounds. The disparity between appearance and reality is implied in these contrasting views and establishes Porter's theme. The family is to meet Great-Aunt Eliza, who represents scientific truth, and both she and science are feared somewhat by Grandmother, who hopes "nothing will happen" when Eliza sets up her telescope.

Before the family sets out, Miranda skips away to her favorite grove of fig trees. She finds a dead baby chicken, and according to the customs of the region, buries it in a tiny grave. Before she leaves, however, she hears a tiny sad voice saying, "Weep, weep." When she is taken away on the journey, she is miserable, thinking she has buried a chicken alive. She associates figs with her misery and rejects those that Aunt Nannie offers her, but she suppresses the misery before they reach Cedar Grove. Miranda's distress surfaces violently when she hears again the "Weep, weep" coming from the ground. In spite of grandmother's fears, it is science that provides balm for Miranda's misery, as Eliza explains the sound as the song of the tree frogs' announcing rain—not at all the sad song of a buried-alive animal.

"The Fig Tree" is a complex story that does not concern Miranda's confrontation with death but rather concerns her awakening to her natural role in life. Miranda's maternal instinct has been apparent in her past visits to the farm. She was fascinated with any little animal as long as "it was a baby and would let her pet and feed it." A part of her self-awareness has been that of the female as the nurturer or life-giver, an awareness that is focused in the fig, a symbol for womb. When Miranda believes she has violated this essential role, she rejects the figs offered as treats, and she "almost forgets" the baby animals at the farm. When Great-Aunt Eliza offers the truth, Miranda is in a fog of bliss. The sound that announces rain is symbolically the sound of life rather than the sound of death.

There is no question that "The Grave" is the most

THE OLD SOUTH

important story in "The Old Order" and perhaps in the whole of the Miranda saga, because it includes the last scene in Miranda's rite of passage, beyond even the events in "Pale Horse, Pale Rider." It is perfect in its compression and execution, and even though it is explained or illuminated by the stories that precede it, it can stand alone. Ostensibly it takes up where "The Fig Tree" left off. Miranda is nine years old, and as the story opens, she is seen with her brother, Paul, who is twelve. The story begins with a paragraph summary of the family's past that centered on "the grandfather" and "the grandmother," confirming again that the viewpoint of the story will be that of children. But this story is less realistic in its details than the previous six stories. It is honed, pared, and shaped in such a way that the events seem placed in a spotlight that illuminates only central details and relegates everything else to peripheral darkness.

The changing of orders is implied in the selling of the land which contained the family graves. Miranda and Paul, who are hunting rabbits and doves, happen upon the empty graves and explore the pits with a sense of adventure and with no fear of the death the graves once contained. They find a gold ring and a silver dove that is a screw head for a coffin. Miranda is drawn to the ring, which represents marriage and a luxurious, aristocratic past, and Paul is drawn to the silver dove, which symbolizes a killing for Paul, the archetypal male as hunter.

When Miranda and Paul leave the cemetery, Paul

shoots a rabbit, which proves to be a female rabbit about to bear young. Miranda has not fully understood life and death and her own relationship to them, and she has not consciously understood her own femaleness, even though she intuited some portion of these truths in "The Fig Tree." Neither she nor Paul can frame the suitable emotion for knowledge of death, having no fear of it because it seems removed from them. The killing of animals likewise induces no horror in Miranda because she does not see the creatures as living things like herself. She sees them only as targets and likes best about hunting the pulling of the trigger and the noise. Miranda's excitement in seeing the bundle of baby rabbits pulled from their dead mother's flesh is not colored with fear or revulsion. She has only "pity and astonishment and a kind of shocked delight in the wonderful little creatures for their own sakes" (366). However, when she sees the blood, she identifies herself with both the female rabbit and the babies and begins to tremble without knowing why; she is "quietly and terribly agitated."

Miranda thinks about "the whole worrisome affair with confused unhappiness for a few days" and then allows it to sink quietly in her mind, where it is "heaped over by accumulated thousands of impressions." When the experience is analyzed at this point, it is a troubling one, unmitigated by a larger perspective. When the memory is resurrected twenty years later, however, as Miranda is picking her way through a market street in a foreign city, it combines with another truth that alters the horror. The memory is pulled from its recesses by Proustian associations when Miranda sees a tray of sugar sweets in the form of baby animals. Not only is the visual experience reminiscent of the long ago embryonic sac of rabbits, but also the olfactory experience of vanilla sweetness and decaying flesh recreates the smells of the cemetery that Miranda and Paul had found before the rabbit was shot. The shooting of the rabbit becomes combined with the discovery of the graves in Miranda's grown-up experienced mind, and thus with the memory that they found treasure in the graves the terrible vision fades and she sees her brother clearly in her mind's eye. In memory, there is whole and eternal truth, the obliteration of time and space. The primary symbols of the story, the grave, the gold ring, the silver dove, and the rabbits, carry the most important meanings. To Miranda the ring suggests comfort and luxury, a life removed from the realities of life and death. But her horrifying association with the rabbits offers the truth of her femaleness, very different from the implied superficial femininity of the ring. It is important that the ring is not a part of the later memory; surviving in the center of the vision is the silver dove, which according to Porter, was a symbol for the holy spirit, or the transcendence over mortality, and it also is a symbol for art, as the Paul of the grown-up Miranda's memory turns it over and over again in his hands with a pleased sober smile.[7]

"Old Mortality"

"Old Mortality," woven around and within the events of "The Grave," was published in the *Southern Review* in 1937. The story is divided into three parts: the first, the longest section, dealing with the past, the second describing a specific incident, and the third assimilating the past and the personal experience of Miranda's present into a meaning. Part I begins with a description of a spirited looking young woman, but the viewpoint soon reveals itself to be that of the woman's nieces who are viewing a photograph of her. Long dead, she sits "forever in the pose of being photographed," fixed like Keats's lovers on the Grecian urn. The nieces, Maria and Miranda, who are twelve and eight, identify their aunt, their father's sister Amy, with a dead past. Her "sad, pretty story from old times" is one among many family legends which Miranda's and Maria's elders enjoy telling. The little girls are disdainful of the unfashionable clothes and backdrops of the ancestral photographs, but they are drawn to them by the mysterious love of the living, who remember and cherish these dead. The tales told about Amy and other ancestors are like bits of poetry, music, or theatre, and through the tales a love of art is being passed on to Maria and Miranda. Amy's story consumes Part I, with only a few digressions to describe other relatives or to reinforce the family's love of the arts. Nostalgically remembered artistic events confirm "for the little girls the nobility of human feeling, the divinity of man's vision of the unseen, the importance of life and death, the depths of the human heart, the romantic value of tragedy" (179). The dangers of such an exclusively sentimental view are presented briefly in Cousin Eva's telling them the story of John Wilkes Booth's assassination of Lincoln and of Miranda's thinking it such a fine dramatic story that it would have been a pleasant part of the family's past had an ancestor seen the event. The haze of sentimentality prevents clear vision, just as distance distorts reality. There are other disparities that Miranda is absorbing even as she accepts them without question; the legends are charming but often untrue, and the poetry expressing the family sentiment is not very good. These half-formed illuminations play an important part in the significant step Miranda takes in Part III.

Part II is set two years later, when Miranda is ten years old and Maria is fourteen, a year after the opening of "The Grave." The beginning refers to vacation on their grandmother's farm, where they discover and read "forbidden reading matter," obviously Gothic novels of the pulp variety, which exploit the protestant fear of Roman Catholicism, even beyond the treatment by Mrs. Radcliffe and Clara Reeve. It is this literature that provides Miranda and Maria with the proper metaphor for their own existence in the Convent of the Child Jesus, the boarding school in New Orleans, where the girls try "to avoid an education" (193). They think of themselves as "immured," like the unlucky heroines of the novels, even though the objective description of the school shows it to be dull rather than sinister. It is an adolescent female state of mind Porter already explored in "Virgin Violeta."

One Saturday their father shows up to take them to the races to see their Uncle Gabriel's mare, Miss Lucy, run. It is to be a momentous event, for Miranda not only will see the whole truth about racing and victory, she also will see the real Uncle Gabriel for the first time. Vastly different from the love-struck beau and hapless husband of Aunt Amy, Gabriel turns out to be "a shabby fat man with bloodshot blue eyes, sad beaten eyes, and a big melancholy laugh, like a groan" (197). Miranda's awakening to truth about victory occurs, interestingly enough, when she sees blood running from Miss Lucy's nose, a parallel to her awakening in "The Grave" when she sees blood on the rabbits. Miranda's reaction to the pitiable horse is to reject victory and to give up her secret ambition to be a jockey. She is "ashamed that she had screamed and shed tears for joy when Miss Lucy, with her bloodied nose and bursting heart, had gone past the judges' stand a neck ahead" (199).

It is a reaction to disillusionment that is visible all along in Miranda's rite of passage: she rejects the circus, the baby animals at the farm, and the experience with the rabbits, rejection here taking the form of burial in the mind. Her proclivity for rejection prepares the reader for further rejection in Part III and in "Pale Horse, Pale Rider," and it parallels the rejection of other protagonists when their ideals prove to be imperfect:

THE OLD SOUTH

Violeta in "Virgin Violeta," Laura in "Flowering Judas," Charles Upton in "The Leaning Tower," and the protagonist of "Theft." It is related to the escape from a reality that is too much to bear, a habit seen in Rosaleen of "The Cracked Looking-Glass," the Thompsons of "Noon Wine," and Mrs. Whipple of "He," who create their own versions of reality in order to escape from truth.

The disillusionment continues when Miranda and Maria are taken to see Miss Honey, Gabriel's melancholy and angry second wife, who is very different from their image of Aunt Amy. The names are significant: Gabriel is not the celestial being of family legend, and his present wife, who looks at Miranda and Maria "as if they were loathsome insects," does not exude honeyed sweetness. Gabriel's calling her "Miss" is a Southern custom, a show of respect that is a carryover from the aristocratic past, and serves only to underline Honey's distance from nobility and grandeur, but Gabriel also has named his exploited horse Miss Lucy. In spite of the disillusionment, the awakening is only partial, and at the end of Part II, when Miranda and Maria return to the convent school, they pick up their romantic game and think of themselves as "immured" for another week. They will not give up their romantic illusions easily, even when confronted with contradictory evidence.

Part III takes place eight years later, when Miranda presumably is eighteen. The familiar journey motif begins this final section, signaling an acquisition of knowledge, even though it stops short of an epiphany.

Miranda is on a train returning to Texas for the funeral of Gabriel, who died in Kentucky but is to be laid to rest beside Amy. On the train Miranda meets Cousin Eva, who was presented briefly in Part I and is a destroyer of illusions. Miranda still is a romantic, although she is modern to the extent that she is dimly fired for women's rights. Having eloped to be married, she continues to believe much of the Amy-Gabriel legend. Cousin Eva, telling her that she must not live in a romantic haze about life, tries to destroy the legend: Amy was not so very beautiful; she probably was pregnant by a stranger, who was killed by Harry, and married Gabriel only in desperation; and she killed herself to avoid disgrace. Eva even reduces the romantic love of the legends to "just sex." Miranda finds herself "deliberately watching a long procession of living corpses, festering women stepping gaily towards the charnel house, their corruption concealed under laces and flowers . . . " (216). Miranda rejects both Eva's version and the romantic version. She rejects her hastily made marriage, and her family rejects her because of her elopement. She is afloat now, free from both the romantic past and the dispassionate, practical present. Ironically, Miranda's father, Harry, and Cousin Eva, who represent opposite attitudes toward the past, are compatible, being perfectly clear about their places in their world. Miranda is at this point clear-headed about her quest. She is the self-acknowledged seeker of truth, while being fully aware for the first time that she does not know what truth is. She asks herself "what is life" and "what is truth" and resolves to know the answers. Truth awaits her during events in "Pale Horse, Pale Rider" and the summarizing scene in "The Grave." Porter confirms Miranda's naïveté and the inconclusiveness of her rite of passage as she closes the story with Miranda's promise to herself that she will "know the truth" at least about what happens to her. Porter says that the promise is made in "hopefulness," in "ignorance."

Miranda's distance from both her father and Eva shows that the breach is a temporal one rather than a philosophical one. They share a bond of common generation, which Miranda cannot. She asks, "Where are my own people and my own time?" (219) and thus echoes the theme of the changing of orders.

Notes

1. Joan Givner, *Katherine Anne Porter: A Life* (New York: Simon and Schuster, 1982) 197.

2. Givner 195.

3. George Hendrick, *Katherine Anne Porter* (New York: Twayne, 1965) 30.

4. William A. Owens, "Regionalism and Universality," *The Texas Literary Tradition: Fiction, Folklore, History,* ed. Don Graham, James W. Lee, and William T. Pilkington (Austin: University of Texas Press, 1983) 69.

5. Charles Kaplan, "True Witness: Katherine Anne Porter," *Colorado Quarterly* 7 (Winter 1959): 323.

6. Kaplan 323.

7. "Recent Southern Fiction: A Panel Discussion," *Bulletin of Wesleyan College* 41 (Jan. 1961) 13.

CHAPTER FOUR

The Rural Southwest

Unlike "The Old Order" and "Old Mortality," other stories Porter set in the rural Southwest have no flavor of the antebellum South. The characters in these stories are New Order people disinterested in the beautiful and fragile legends of the past. Their concerns are practical. The Whipples ("He") and the Thompsons ("Noon Wine") are poor whites struggling for acceptance in the respectable middle class; Granny Weatherall thought her years of hard work would bring her old-age satisfaction and a sense of order; Stephen's family ("The Downward Path to Wisdom") are materially prosperous in the New Order that ignores spiritual richness; and the Müllers in "Holiday" typify hardworking immigrants single-minded in their industry. Written during the years Porter was planning and writing the Miranda saga, these stories represent another facet of the childhood experience she was mining, a facet at once less personal to her and less conducive to myth. They exhibit a particular thematic grimness and power that evolve from her treatment of despair and from her examination of families in which love and compassion have held no place, a variation of her theme of betrayal.

The effectiveness of this body of fiction is enhanced by the presence of memorable characters similar to Flannery O'Connor's grotesques, the idiot boy in "He," the mysterious Helton in "Noon Wine," and the mute Ottilie in "Holiday," and by a concentration of some of Porter's familiar stylistic devices. Animals are part of the background in these rural stories, and animal imagery consequently functions in an especially important way. The journey motif common in Porter's canon is used here with particular irony. "He" concludes with the bewildered and self-pitying Mrs. Whipple's making the trip with her son to the County Home. "The Jilting of Granny Weatherall" includes Granny's dreaming of stepping up in a cart driven by Death to begin her last journey, one that concludes in despair. In "Noon Wine" the Thompsons' excursions into the countryside at the end of the story dramatically illustrate the last desperate attempts of Mr. Thompson to gain respectability, the controlling motive to all his actions and the subject of the story. Stephen's car journey home with Mama at the end of "The Downward Path to Wisdom" symbolizes the acquisition of horrible knowledge summarized in the grim little song of hate. Only at the end of "Holiday" does the journey at the end of the story lead to an uplifting vision.

THE RURAL SOUTHWEST

"He"

"He," published in *New Masses* in 1927, was the first of the rural Southwestern stories to appear. From the beginning of the story the tone is bitter to the point of sarcasm. One of the stylistic methods Porter uses to create irony here is to follow seemingly straight-forward statements with a comment or modifier that undermines the accuracy of the statements and establishes a paradox, almost as if the first statements were paraphrases of what one of the characters, usually Mrs. Whipple, has said, and the follow-up comment a perspective by the all-wise author establishing balance. For example, in the first paragraph, the narrative reads, "Mrs. Whipple was all for taking what was sent and calling it good," a statement that no doubt represents Mrs. Whipple's often expressed pious philosophy of life, but the sentence is completed with a detracting clause, "anyhow when the neighbors were in earshot" (49). Mrs. Whipple's concern for the neighbors' opinion is reinforced immediately as the paragraph ends with her saying to her husband, "Nobody's going to get a chance to look down on us."

Mrs. Whipple's hypocrisy is shared by Mr. Whipple, who worries that his wife's public announcements of love for their simpleminded son, referred to only as "He," will make people think that the father has no feelings for the son. But Mr. Whipple plays a secondary role in the drama, for it is the mother's story primarily, establishing a common motif in these stories of mothers' roles in family life. Mrs. Whipple's concern with appearance never abates in the story. When her brother and his family come to visit, she kills the pig that later would have brought much needed money, only in order to impress her relatives, whom she considers "refined." Finally, when Mrs. Whipple accompanies her simple-minded son to the County Home, she wears her best dress because "she couldn't stand to go looking like charity" (58).

Mrs. Whipple's representation of Him to the neighbors is an attempt to create a better image of the family. She describes Him as mischievous, good-natured, obedient, "able as any other child," and protected by God above or a guardian angel. But privately she resents His eating food that might have gone to the two normal children, whom she gives warmer clothes and His blanket that He does not need because "He sets around the fire a lot" (54). "He" takes care of the bees because He "don't really mind" if He gets a sting; He is sent to snatch the baby pig from its ma, "a great fighter," because "He's not scared," and He is sent for a dangerous bull because He is "steady around animals" (55).

Irony is implicit in the distance between the ideal of mother love and Mrs. Whipple's disdain for "Him," between a selfless love declared by the mother and the total self-absorption that underlies her concern with appearance and is revealed in all its horror at the end of the story, when in her guilt she interprets His tears as

THE RURAL SOUTHWEST

accusations against her, completely missing (as Hardy points out) the possibility that His tears are an expression of love for her or a normal human reaction to being separated from His family, no matter how odious they are.[1]

Hendrick has noted that the name "Whipple" suggests a whip, indicating the family's being whipped by the circumstances of their lives, some of which circumstances they create or nourish in their ignorance, their mind-set for poverty and failure, and their obsessive attention to social appearances.[2] That the reader never knows the given names of Mr. and Mrs. Whipple is a reminder that their relationship to the others in the story is distant and superficial. Adna and Emly, the other two Whipple children, and Alfy, their cousin, are named, as is one of the neighbors, Jim Ferguson. Every other character in the story is unnamed, including Mrs. Whipple's brother, his plump healthy wife, the doctor who comes to see Him, and the neighbor who drives Mrs. Whipple and Him to the County Home. Porter's emerging technique of using a range of specificity of names to give relative values to her characters or to define their thematic roles is clearly illustrated in this story. "He" becomes a much more complex name in the story than it appears at first. Because no one in the story, including the doctor, calls Him by his given name, He does not have a human identity. The name "He" identifies only his gender and is in contrast to "Adna" and "Emly," names that show the opposite way they are regarded by their mother. The capitalizing of "He" shows that the pronoun has come to be his name, but it also ironically suggests the Deity and draws the reader's attention to the great distance between Mrs. Whipple's surface piety and her un-Christian treatment of her idiot son. Mrs. Whipple's failure to see Him as human is integrated into her obsessive concern with appearance. He is treated like an animal, and it is no wonder he identifies with the baby pig (who screeches "like a baby in a tantrum" when He snatches it from its ma) when Mrs. Whipple slices its throat. Like Miranda, who knows something about herself when she sees the blood on the baby rabbits, when He sees the blood after the butchering, He gives "a great jolting breath," runs away, and refuses to come into the dining room where the baby pig, "roasted to a crackling," sits "in the middle of the table, full of dressing, a pickled peach in his mouth and plenty of gravy for the sweet potatoes" (53).

Porter illustrates poignantly in "He" that love is necessary for children to become fully realized humans. If the reader adds to that view Porter's implication in "The Grave" that humans have to recognize their animal natures, the essential truths of Porter's philosophy can be seen in a humanistic sequence. One must first recognize his or her animal self, and then one must be the recipient of love, a somewhat deterministic view. If a child is not loved, then he or she is forever doomed to a heartless existence. "He" has a line of descendants in Porter's fiction, two more of whom are in this group of stories. They are all related to Ninette in "Magic."

THE RURAL SOUTHWEST

"The Jilting of Granny Weatherall"

The human rights of Him were betrayed by his mother's refusal or inability to love him. In "The Jilting of Granny Weatherall," published in 1929 in *transition*, the theme of betrayal although different is equally important. The story is based in part on the death of Porter's grandmother Catherine Anne Skaggs Porter, who was the model for the grandmother of "The Old Order." The social level of Granny Weatherall is higher than that of the Whipples partly because laziness and obsessive concern with appearance are not among her personal traits. Her past included hard times, or as she recalls, "a hard pull, but not too much for her" (83). The meaning of "The Jilting of Granny Weatherall" is ambiguous. Although Granny's deathbed memories keep dredging up the humiliating and traumatic event, the focal point of the story is not the jilting of Granny in her girlhood by her fiancé George, who failed to show up for the wedding. It is rather the disillusionment with which Granny ends her life. It is the most horrifying of Porter's stories because it calls into question the value of an ordinary religious life. Granny identifies the bridegroom George with the bridegroom Christ of the parable and as she dies declares that the second bridegroom, Christ, has not appeared, that God has not sent the sign she expected, and that this grief wipes all other sorrow away.

This story is skillfully executed in a stream of consciousness mode, with Porter's retaining Granny's viewpoint and realistically depicting the musings of a mind barely connected to its physical moorings. Time is suspended, and the past and the present are blended. Granny's mind functions by free association, making connections between perceived images of the present and memories of the past. Her fading senses distort her perceptions; she thinks Doctor Harry floats and imagines ants are in her bed. She is losing her sense of self, confusing herself with one of her children named Hapsy.

Porter's theme of betrayal here contains irony. It is not so much that Granny's religion betrayed her, or that specifically God or Christ betrayed her in the way that the faithless George betrayed her long ago, but rather that she betrayed herself by establishing illusions of an ordered life. She imagined that life was a plan, whose edges could be tucked in orderly; she has followed the rules of the Church (she "went to Holy Communion last week"), and she has adhered to a series of precepts such as "You waste life when you waste good food." Granny also sought fulfillment through visible order: "It was good to have everything clean and folded away, with the hair brushes and tonic bottles sitting straight on the white embroidered linen . . . and the pantry shelves laid out with rows of jelly glasses . . . " (81).

Two of Porter's most important canonical symbols and images appear in this story, the images of light and dark, which become symbols, and the journey metaphor. When Granny's eyes close, it is like "a dark curtain drawn around the bed" (81). She remembers a fog

rising over the valley and the children's fear of the ensuing darkness. She remembers dark smoke obscuring
the orchard, and the smoke becomes mingled with the
thought of hell, which she identifies as the state of her
life when she was left at the altar. Shadows, fog, and
smoke represent physical reality, betrayal, death, and
hell all at once. Light, on the other hand, represents
happiness, hope, and life. Granny recalls that the long-
ago fog had required the light of lamps, which had been
beautiful and had alleviated both the darkness and the
children's fear. When she dies, blowing out the light,
she is relinquishing not only life but also hope, giving
way to "the endless darkness" that will "curl around
the light and swallow it up" (89).

Granny imagines near the end that she is stepping
up into a cart driven by Death, but in fact her whole
dying reverie has taken the form of a journey as she
wanders into the past recalling both griefs and joys, as
well as hardships. She has "to go a long way back
through a great many rooms to find Hapsy," and she
also makes "a long journey outward, looking for
Hapsy," suggesting that Hapsy already has died.
Granny imagines Hapsy's saying, "I thought you'd
never come" and "you haven't changed a bit" (85-86).
Porter's provision of only sketchy information about
Hapsy, as well as Granny's other children, allows her to
remain faithful to the stream-of-consciousness technique and to illuminate the most important aspects of
Granny's final day.

The Biblical allusion to the parable of the virgins

and the lighting of the lamps underlies the story (Matthew 25:1-13). In Granny's version, she herself has been among the dutiful virgins, but the inconstant George has supplanted Christ and distorts the parable. The jilting of Granny cost her her faith, the "something not given back" by her marriage to the good man John.

"Noon Wine"

Faith also is absent in the religious attitudes of the Thompsons of "Noon Wine," who rely on Protestant fundamentalism as a means to respectability. "Noon Wine," first published in *Story* in 1937, is on the surface an uncomplicated story about murder and its consequences, with the characters of the Thompsons and their rural neighbors realistic representatives of back-country values and society. But the story raises certain questions, the answers to which are crucial to an understanding of the story. The central question is why Thompson kills Hatch.

In order to answer that question the reader has to understand the symbolic values of Helton and Hatch, who are displayed against the Thompsons' realism, and the relationships among all the main characters. Olaf Helton is the first to appear in the story as he approaches the Thompson farm to ask for work. He seems ghostly from the start: "His eyes sat in his head and let things pass by them" (223), he seems "to be sleeping with his eyes open" (224), and he speaks "as from the tomb" (224) or "grudgingly from the darkness" (231). He is referred to by Mrs. Thompson as "a disembodied spirit" (236) and by the Thompson sons as "Brother Bones" (242). While these descriptions and appellations point to the mystery that surrounds him, they also suggest his symbolic relationship to death. Figuratively, Helton is a dead man, simply waiting for law and order to catch up with him, just as he brings death indirectly to other characters.

Royal Earle Thompson is a realistic representative of his class and place. He is "a noisy proud man" who holds "his neck so straight his whole face" stands "level with his Adam's apple" (222). He divides chores into men's work, hired men's work, and woman's work, "all his carefully limited fields of activity . . . related somehow to Mr. Thompson's feeling for the appearance of things, his own appearance in the sight of God and man. 'It don't look right,' was his final reason for not doing anything he did not wish to do" (233). His pretentious name is a sign of his appreciation for appearance, and he does appear to be a solid citizen who pays his taxes, contributes to the preacher's salary, owns land, and heads a family. The truth is that he is shiftless and lazy. Homer T. Hatch represents a different kind of man. He is a cunning and indefatigable pursuer of human bounty under the guise of law and order. As he says, "The law is solidly behind me." Hatch is described, from Thompson's viewpoint, in unpleasant images: a fat man, he has tobacco-stained teeth and a droopy look in his "wicked" eyes.

In developing the characters of the three men, Porter makes sanity a moral issue. Although Helton is insane by any standard, having murdered his brother for borrowing (and losing) his harmonica, are Thompson and Hatch necessarily "sane"? Thompson illustrates the subjectivity of the label when he defends Helton: "He never acted crazy to me . . . He always acted like a sensible man, to me. He never got married, for one thing, and he works like a horse, and I bet he's got the first cent I paid him when he landed here, and he don't drink, an he never says a word, much less swear, and he don't waste time runnin' around Saturday nights, and if he's crazy, . . . why, I think I'll go crazy myself for a change" (247). Thompson is disregarding Helton's strangeness and saying that Helton is an industrious, thrifty, sober bachelor who is Thompson's opposite, in many respects his ideal. Hatch himself observes, paraphrasing Thompson, "There ain't every man in a strait jacket that ought to be there" (250). The relationships among the three men must be defined in order to discern the story's meaning. Because Thompson is the center of interest, the most important relationships are his to Helton and his to Hatch. Thompson shares with Helton insanity or its latency (his Aunt Ida was in the state asylum), but beyond that they are bound together by Thompson's dependence on Helton for his economic survival. Thompson's relationship to Hatch is different. They share many personality traits, as the narrator points out: both are noisy men who shout and guffaw at their own jokes, and both are law-abiding. But to

Thompson, Hatch represents his own worst self; he continuously thinks that Hatch looks familiar to him, and he regards him with dislike from the beginning. When Thompson describes his wife's invalidism and expensive operations, Hatch says, "It's just as you say: a dead loss, keepin' one of 'em up" (248), not at all what Thompson has said but perhaps what he meant.

Underscoring the bonds among the men is Porter's use of the "foreigner"/"stranger" label to make a paradoxical point: basic human nature is shared by everyone, but ignorant of this, each person feels isolated. Thompson first says to Helton, "You're a forriner ain't you?" (225). Mrs. Thompson calls Helton "the stranger," and Hatch, who is described as "the stranger" from the moment he appears at the Thompson farm, in turn calls Thompson "stranger." At the end of the story, Herbert, the younger son, stares at his father "like a stranger" (267). One truth is, of course, that human nature has a common wellspring.[3]

All the characters act from subconscious motives or misguided intentions, irrational impulses illustrated by Porter's repeated use of images of blindness, light, and animals. Mrs. Thompson is particularly unseeing; bolstered as she is by her pious adherence to fundamentalist strictures, she misses her own similarity to Hatch, whose "rabbit teeth" link him to Mrs. Thompson, who is described in rabbit images. Animal images exist in verbs (Thompson brays, Arthur bawls) and in descriptions of the characters and their actions (Hatch, whose eyes are pig-like, looks like the cat that ate the canary, and Thompson brings the ax down on Hatch "as if he were stunning a beef"). Porter again implies that humans must first recognize their animal natures before they can be redeemed by love. The Thompsons are a long distance from such awareness, much less from redemption.

The question about the motivation of the murder remains. That Thompson's killing of Hatch is subconsciously motivated is proved by his inability to remember exactly what happened. Thompson believes that Hatch attacks Helton with a bowie knife, a fantasy that represents Thompson's belief that Hatch is a threat to his own well-being, ensured by the farm's prosperity that Helton in turn guarantees. Thompson's killing of Hatch can be seen clearly as Thompson's attempt to save himself and his family from economic ruin. On the other hand, since Hatch represents to Thompson his dark self, killing him can be construed as his attempt to kill off the side of himself that he despises. What seems clear is that Thompson does not kill Hatch, as Harry John Mooney, Jr., suggests, in a heroic effort to save Helton because Helton is a better man that the odious Hatch.[4] While the psychological motivation obviously has some strength, other evidence in the story suggests that it is the need for economic survival that is the stronger force. The title of the story refers to the song that Helton plays on his harmonica and that Hatch explains as being about feeling so good you drink all your "likker" before noon and have none when you need it after the work is done; it is a song that describes

THE RURAL SOUTHWEST

Thompson's self-indulgence and explains his middle-age apathy which works against his desire to maintain a good appearance in the eyes of his neighbors. Such an emphasis is given to Thompson's concern with appearance that the motive seems even more clear. It also explains Thompson's suicide at the end of the story. With Helton dead, the farm's decay is sure, and with his good name gone, as well as the moral support of his family, Thompson has no choice but death.

Warren singled out "Noon Wine" to illustrate Porter's powerful imagination, which he said could be best understood "if we appreciate its essential austerity, its devotion to the fact drenched in God's direct daylight, its concern with the inwardness of character, and its delight in the rigorous and discriminating deployment of a theme."[5] To illustrate, he quotes a description of Mr. Thompson in the story:

Mr. Thompson was a tough weather-beaten man with stiff black hair and a week's growth of black whiskers. He was a noisy proud man who held his neck so straight his whole face stood level with his Adam's apple, and the whiskers continued down his neck and disappeared into a black thatch under his open collar. The churn rumbled and swished like the belly of a trotting horse, and Mr. Thompson seemed somehow to be driving a horse with one hand, reining it in and urging it forward; and every now and then he turned halfway around and squirted a tremendous spit of tobacco juice out over the steps. The door stones were brown and gleaming with fresh tobacco juice. (222)

In the "ordinariness" of the items presented—the trotting motion of the churn, the swish of the milk, the tobacco juice—Warren finds Porter's power of isolating common things so that they glow in relief and serve to explain as well as to foreshadow Thompson's tragic end. The prideful Thompson would rather be holding the reins of a spirited horse than the cord of a churn, and in images and figures of speech Porter conveys Thompson's capacity for play-acting and avoiding reality. Thompson spits his tobacco juice as a masculine protest against fate and, according to Warren, sets the stage for the arrival of Helton, whom Thompson will keep at any cost in order to avoid work he considers womanly and degrading and to defend the picture of himself.[6]

"The Downward Path to Wisdom"

The Thompsons' encounter with irrational forces has defeated them rather than enlightened them, and Porter continues to present characters who are not edified by the knowledge gained from life's experiences. Such a character is Stephen in "The Downward Path to Wisdom," published in *Harper's Bazaar* in 1939. Four-year-old Stephen is one of Porter's child-victims who are destroyed morally because love has not tempered the animal nature. What Stephen has learned is rejection, to which his response is hate, and as his name indicates, he is a martyr to human cruelty. Understandably, animal imagery is important in this story, as Stephen's animal self is depicted. The theme of betrayal is dominant, but there is no self-betrayal here because Stephen is not old enough to consciously choose his delusions. Rather, all the adults betray him. He is sent from the quarreling parents to Grandmother, whose house should have been a refuge from faithlessness and disloyalty but is not, and then back to Mama, who already has rejected him. Mooney says that the ultimate betrayal "represents a kind of tacit conspiracy on the part of his elders to defeat the forces of love and hope in the child, and to bring him to an unwise and precocious maturity," which, "when it comes, is one of cynicism and disillusionment; childhood is surrendered, but nothing is gained."[7]

Balloons are an important symbol in the story, associated as they are with childhood, carnivals, springtime, and birthday parties. In Stephen's story, they become much more. The balloons that Uncle David gives to Stephen have advertising on them and thus have a purpose other than a festive one. They also become a means to popularity for Stephen, who, wanting to ingratiate himself with his school friend Frances, brings all the balloons to her. When she comes to visit, they blow up balloons again, Stephen significantly choosing an "apple-colored" one, which according to Hendrick is an allusion to Adam and Eve.[8] He takes further risks to please Frances when he sneaks a lemon, sugar, and a china teapot to make lemonade for himself and Frances in a scene suggestive of the Garden of Eden, redolent with both sexual and religious imagery. In the midst of it Old Janet, Grandmother's servant, comes to accuse Stephen of theft, his sin in the eyes of the adults, who banish him to his mother. Stephen's sleepy song as Mama drives away with him is the natural result of his betrayal and his experience: "I hate Papa, I hate Mama, I hate Grandma . . . " (387).

"Holiday"

No one in "The Downward Path to Wisdom," "Noon Wine," "The Jilting of Granny Weatherall," or "He" awakens to moral understanding, but that it not true of "Holiday." Porter said of "Holiday" in the preface to her *Collected Stories* (1965) that it represented one of her prolonged struggles "with a human situation" she was too young to cope with at the time it occurred. The version that appeared in 1960 in the *Atlantic Monthly* had been written twenty-five years earlier, in the midst of her writing of the Miranda cycle. It shares with the Miranda stories, and others with an autobiographical center, a protagonist whose experience in the story takes her another step further toward knowing something about the universe.

The Müllers, a German family depicted in "Holiday," are characteristic of the German immigrants Porter knew in the region around Kyle, Texas. The event that inspired this story was, according to Givner, a visit Porter and her sister Gay made in their teens.[9] Like "He,"

THE RURAL SOUTHWEST

"Noon Wine," "The Cracked Looking-Glass," and *Ship of Fools*, it contains an aberrant personality, a grotesque who is the agent by which knowledge is made available. In this case, the narrator indeed learns an important although subtle truth.

The first climax of the story occurs when the narrator realizes that the mute and deformed Ottilie actually is one of the Müller children. Because she could not function in the defined role of wife, mother, sister, or daughter, the Müllers had relegated her to the role of servant, peripheral to the family. The narrator, however, justifies the exclusion by asking "What else could they have done with Ottilie?" She promises herself that she will forget her, too. The final climax, the most important one, occurs when the initial discovery is extended into a more important meaning. When Mother Müller dies and the other family members set out for the funeral, Ottilie begins howling in a frenzy. The narrator, concluding that Ottilie is expressing grief at being denied participation in the mourning ceremony, hitches a wagon and starts out for the burial with Ottilie at her side. An important preliminary step is reached when the narrator accidentally touches Ottilie's bare flesh and is so shocked at her own sense of Ottilie's "realness, her humanity, this shattered being that was a woman," that "a howl as doglike and despairing as her own rose . . . unuttered and died again, to be a perpetual ghost" (434). Thereafter Ottilie's face is "grotesquely changed" and she laughs out, clapping her hands for joy. The narrator believes that the feeling of the sun, the bright air, "the jolly senseless staggering" of the wagon wheels, and "the peacock green of the heavens" had reached Ottilie. In other words, Ottilie's senses that confirm physical existence were awakened, and Ottilie was responding to the awakening. The puzzle in this story is not why Ottilie laughs with happiness on the way to her mother's funeral but rather what the narrator learns from it all.

The narrator ponders her original mistakes, first to assume that Ottilie could be explained in ordinary human terms, and second to assume that there was something she could do for Ottilie. And yet the mere act of trying to bridge the distance between herself and Ottilie has led her to this truth. Ottilie is not part of a discernible order. She is inexplicable, like life itself. The narrator will not try to put Ottilie within the context of a limited perspective but rather will allow her to remain ineffable. Together they will celebrate the heat of the sun, the fact of life, on this most religious of days, a true holy day, that affirms human life and the mystery of it. The title of the story assumes its most important meaning.

Notes

1. John Edward Hardy, *Katherine Anne Porter* (New York: Frederick Ungar, 1973) 38.

2. George Hendrick, *Katherine Anne Porter* (New York: Twayne, 1965) 84.

3. See Thomas F. Walsh, "Deep Similarities in 'Noon Wine,' " *Mosaic* 9.1 (1975): 83–91.

4. Harry J. Mooney, Jr., *The Fiction and Criticism of Katherine Anne Porter* (Pittsburgh: University of Pittsburgh Press, 1962) 42.

5. Robert Penn Warren, Introduction, "Katherine Anne Porter: A Critical Bibliography," by Edward T. Schwartz, *Bulletin of the New York Public Library* 57 (1953): 213.

6. Warren 213.

7. Mooney 52.

8. Hendrick 98.

9. Joan Givner, *Katherine Anne Porter: A Life* (New York: Simon and Schuster, 1982) 98.

CHAPTER FIVE

New England and Greenwich Village

During the last half of the 1920s, Porter lived in Connecticut, New York, and Salem, married and divorced an Englishman named Ernest Stock, and met Caroline Gordon, Robert Penn Warren, and Josephine Herbst, all important literary acquaintances. While at this time she was mining the region of her childhood for stories like "He" and "The Jilting of Granny Weatherall," she also was exploring in fiction her immediate environment, both personal and social, producing stories decidedly different from those of the Southwest.

"Rope," "Theft," "The Cracked Looking-Glass," and "A Day's Work" are set in the New England countryside and New York City, and they are variations on a theme of failed male-female relationships. "Rope" illustrates the illogical hate that lies under the surface of a marriage; "Theft" depicts a young woman's gradual awareness that apathy has prevented her finding love; "The Cracked Looking-Glass" examines a May-December marriage in which the wife finds fulfillment only in the fantasies she creates; and "A Day's Work" dramatizes the conflicts in a loveless marriage further beset by the economic problems of the Depression.

"Rope"

"Rope," the first story Porter wrote reflecting her mature experience, was published in *The Second American Caravan* in 1928. It was written near the end of her brief marriage to Ernest Stock, and it reveals the connection between the surface, incidental bickering of a husband and wife and the deeper, more serious breaking apart of their union. Mooney describes the two levels of the story: "Read in one way, it is a diverting social comedy with a happy ending, and, read in another, it is a disturbing revelation of the malice stored beneath the blandest surfaces of life."[1]

The first and last paragraphs of "Rope" present idyllic scenes, framing a bitter quarrel between an unnamed husband and wife and providing a standard against which the relationship is measured. As in other Porter stories, vague allusions to the Bible or literature help define the ideal that exposes the emptiness of the present experience. The first sentence illustrates how Porter's classical style depends on the shock value of the periodic sentence. It begins with "On the third day," a phrase that the reader should link to "He arose from the dead" in the Bible, an essential statement in Christian theology that confirms the validity of the spiritual life. But Porter's sentence ends with the puzzling clause "he came . . . back . . . carrying . . . a twenty-four-yard coil of rope," which conjures up images of violence or work. The question of why he bought the rope is never truly answered, but discerning the symbolic meaning of the rope is necessary to an understanding of the story.

He says he thought they might use it "to hang clothes on, or something," but she points out that they already have a fifty-foot line "right before his eyes." Clearly the rope means something different to each of them. For the husband, it symbolizes masculine country work, which he, a vacationing city dweller, has little understanding of. However, his refusal to exchange it at the store for something more practical represents his attempt at asserting himself in his marriage. To the wife the rope symbolizes his impracticality and lack of cooperation in domestic matters. As the story progresses, however, the rope comes to mean more than these early subjective representations. Critics have suggested that the rope is the marriage itself, which is unraveling, and that Porter is hinting at various puns on marriage such as "tying the knot," the "tie that binds," and "being roped in." In her essay "The Necessary Enemy," Porter provides an important clue to the symbolism of the rope. She says that both love and hate are natural, interwoven parts of every human relationship and that marriage is no exception. To illustrate her point, she describes a hypothetical lovers' quarrel that is an abstract summary of the quarrel in "Rope."[2] The rope then is the intertwining of love and hate that make up a marriage. Nance points out that in "Rope" it is the disproportion between effect, the bitter quarrel, and apparent cause, the purchase of the rope, which draws attention to the story's major theme, "the awareness of free-floating hatred in marriage."[3] Porter's method of presenting the dialogue indirectly in this story is the most startling of its technical effects. Nance maintains correctly that an important effect of the technique is the impression that the author is constantly present and "providing a steady line of reference by which each evil and irrational word of the characters judges itself."[4]

The final paragraph, which describes an illogical return to a former idyllic state, without the issue of the rope resolved, contains an apparent allusion to one of Whitman's most beautiful and spiritual poems, "Out of the Cradle Endlessly Rocking."[5] In the poem a "he-bird" whose mate has died sings a succession of arias that reflect the stages of his spiritual understanding and acceptance of death. One of the most poignant of the arias is sung by the still hopeful he-bird calling desperately upon the elements to bring back the "she-bird." The she of "Rope" reduces a whippoorwill's out-of-season song to the vulgar speculation that "maybe his girl stood him up" (48), showing the reader in the final paragraph the disparity between the heroic and the trivial, the ideal and the actual, and also the delusion with which the wife is regarding the marriage.

"Theft"

"Theft," published in *The Gyroscope* in 1929, shares with "Rope" an unspecified setting and a negative atmosphere, although the setting of "Theft" is urban and the narrative unfolds from a retrospective and restricted viewpoint. Inspired by Porter's years in Greenwich Village in the twenties, this complex story is puzzling in the ambiguity of its conclusion and the symbolic meaning of the purse. If, however, the story is read with an understanding of Porter's views on apathy and her treatment of self-betrayal in other stories, and if the function of the religious imagery and symbolism is properly identified, the story's meaning emerges clearly. The story begins with the unnamed protagonist's discovering that her purse, a birthday gift from a former lover, was stolen from her apartment. Most of the remainder of the story is told in retrospect, as the woman reconstructs the events of the preceding day that led up to her discovery of the theft. The retrospective events involve her relationships with four men, Camilo, Roger, Bill, and Eddie. Each has represented an unsatisfactory love relationship. Camilo lives by impractical, romantic standards; Roger will be reconciled with a woman named Stella; the self-pitying and self-indulgent Bill has cheated the protagonist out of money; and the missing Eddie has finally ended the relationship that he implies in his letter the protagonist had already destroyed.

In recounting the events that preceded the discovery of the missing purse, the protagonist realizes that the janitress stole the purse. Her first thought is that getting it back will be impossible, and she decides to let it go. But there arises "in her blood a deep almost murderous anger." Under an emotional compulsion that is separate from her will, the narrator descends to the domain of the janitress and asks for the purse back, pointing out that it has a sentimental value only to her. After swearing that she "never laid eyes on" the purse, the janitress finally admits she took it for her niece, who "needs a pretty purse," and makes the protagonist feel guilty for reclaiming it. In an ironic reversal, in a Dantesque scene that suggests an awakening to knowledge, the protagonist sees herself as thief of her own purse and by association extends her culpability to all her other losses. She sees that by her will-less and apathetic existence, she has stolen life from herself.

The religious structure of descent and ascent, the prevalence of the mystical number three, and the meaning of the tableaux the protagonist and Roger observe during their wild taxi ride through the rain-drenched city have enabled the protagonist to infer some truth about her existence. The night before, she talked to three men, and three boys walk in front of her and Roger's taxi. The three boys are arguing, albeit in vulgar terms, about the relative merits of sacred and profane love. Roger apathetically rejects both extremes. In another scene two girls run by, one of them complaining in self-pity. Roger represents a will-less position; Bill is self-pitying like the girl; and Camilo, whom the protagonist had left earlier in the evening, lives by a code of romantic love like one of the adolescent boys. Only Eddie, who is known merely by the memory of the protagonist and a letter she receives from him, seems to have offered the woman a love that was real; according to the letter, she destroyed the love, and he has decided that it is "not worth all this abominable. . . . " The protagonist's failure to claim her possessions, all of which are represented by the purse, is her representative stance in her apathetic existence. She and all her friends of the modern wasteland are hollow people of the twentieth century, substituting ritual and withdrawal for commitment and vitality. It is important that they all try to escape the rain, a symbol of growth and renewal, and that coffee and alcohol are the communal potions of their false sacrament, their religion of non-life.

"The Cracked Looking-Glass"

Religion is a visible part of the lives of Porter's Irish Catholics in New England. "The Cracked Looking-Glass," published in *Scribner's Magazine* in 1932, was in-

spired by a story Porter heard while she was living in a
Connecticut farmhouse and involved a widow who was
talked about because she kept young boys in her home.[6]
The story intrigued Porter for many years before she
was able to produce it in a form satisfactory to her for
publication. "The Cracked Looking-Glass" takes as its
most important theme illusion versus reality, and the
cracked looking-glass is the central symbol of the story,
providing the clue for the only defensible interpretation
of the conclusion. Rosaleen had been a fine, lusty girl
when Dennis, widowed and thirty years her senior, had
courted her. According to natural sequence, Rosaleen's
youthful animal energy should have been channeled
into motherhood, but the only child she and Dennis
had, a boy, died within two days of birth. Dennis has
long since ceased to be either a proper husband or lover
to Rosaleen, and at the beginning of the story Rosaleen
is not content to let Dennis replace the dead son. She
has sublimated both her sexual energy and her maternal instinct in storytelling, often taking the form of
dream interpretation or of reliving her youthful past,
and in ambiguous liaisons with young men.

Rosaleen has created illusions by which she lives
because her present reality is intolerable. Since motherhood has been denied her, Rosaleen fantasizes about
her girlhood, remembering the parties and feast days
and the boys who chased her during her triumphant
maidenhood in Ireland. She still wears bright colors
and worries about the curl in her red hair, and she can
deceive herself as long as she does not look into a clear

mirror. The looking-glass she has is cracked across its center (suggesting the two opposing personalities of maiden and mother in Rosaleen), and while the glass may cause her to look like "a monster," Rosaleen is comforted by knowing that the image is a distortion. The looking-glass allows her fantasy about her unchanged looks to flourish. DeMouy describes Rosaleen's dilemma: "Undefined as a mother, Rosaleen is essentially a maiden caught on the other side of mid-life with only the dry laurels of her successful girlhood to drape around her head."[7]

Rosaleen's relationships with the three young men in the story illustrate the confused identity. The most important of the young men was Kevin, who has been gone for several years when the story begins. An important passage illustrates the young men's role in Rosaleen's life. When she thinks of the "fine man" Dennis was when she first knew him, before his "getting old . . . took the heart out of" her, his image becomes Kevin's, and when she thinks of her dead son and the fine young man he might have become, his image also becomes Kevin's. DeMouy concludes, "As both Prince Charming and son, he admits both sides of Rosaleen's personality."[8] Hugh Sullivan in Boston and the dull-witted neighbor boy, in progressively more desperate substitutions, offer her the same kind of sublimation.

The journey Rosaleen makes to Boston to find her sister Honora was instigated in Rosaleen's subconscious to bolster the illusions which are the breath of life for her. The trip itself is an external form of the escape from reality she has been practicing. Rosaleen says that she has learned in a dream that Honora is dying and that she must go to her. She will also use the trip to buy a new coat and a new mirror to replace the cracked one. The journey occurs in two parts, the first from Connecticut to New York, where Rosaleen looks at beautiful lingerie as a form of sexual fantasizing, cries through two romantic movies, eats chocolate and ice cream, and goes to pray for Honora in a church richly dressed in candles and flowers and the fragrance of incense. It is a nostalgic grasping for the past, a journey backward to a romantic state like that of Virgin Violeta or the young Miranda of "Old Mortality." In spite of the serious purpose of the trip, the first part is devoid of unpleasant reality; it is instead a pleasure trip filled with a feast-day atmosphere and an adolescent romantic haze. For the moment, Rosaleen seems to have recaptured her girlhood.

From New York Rosaleen boards a boat that will carry her overnight to Boston. After this night sea journey, which DeMouy sees as a symbolic journey to the land of the dead, Rosaleen arrives in Boston where harsh realities await her in the discovery that Honora does not live there and in her encounter with the sly young man Hugh Sullivan, who misses Rosaleen's maternal interest in him ("You might be Kevin or my own brother, or my own little lad alone in the world") and sees only her sexual interest.[9] He rejects her offer to return to Connecticut to live with her and Dennis, explaining that he was "caught at it once in Dublin" with "a fine woman like yourself . . . and her husband peeking through a crack in the wall the whole time" (128).

From the perspective of Boston, home and Dennis look good, and Rosaleen flees a harsher reality to a more comfortable one with which she has already dealt. Critical controversy over the story's meaning has centered on the ending. Hardy, for example, sees the conclusion as distinctly positive, as Rosaleen's relinquishing her dreams and resigning herself to her marriage.[10] But DeMouy sees the ending differently. She says that "in rejecting tales and dreams Rosaleen does not turn toward truth but toward another kind of fantasy—maybe Kevin will return to her after all."[11] Proof that Rosaleen has not had a true awakening lies in several more details. She "forgot" to buy a new looking-glass, one that would have removed the monster from her vision but also would have revealed a reality she was not ready to accept. She lies to Dennis about Honora, and after supporting the dim-witted local boy's story of ghosts, declaring she has seen the same phenomenon many times, she tells the boy, "Eat your supper now, and sleep here the night; ye can't go out by your lone and the Evil waiting for ye" (130). She beds him down in Kevin's room, an act that suggests he is another replacement for Kevin. At the very end of the story, Rosaleen mothers Dennis, who is all she has for the moment. The reader is left, however, with the impression that Rosaleen's reduction is temporary. While she has said she doesn't have the respect she once had for dreams, she still has her cracked looking-glass and there will be other young men.

"A Day's Work"

In "A Day's Work," published in *Nation* in 1940, Porter expands her view of Irish Catholic immigrants. Porter got the idea for this story from a quarrel she overheard through the ventilator ducts in her Greenwich Village apartment building in the 1920s.[12] Set in the slums of New York during the depression, "A Day's Work" focuses on another husband and wife in a soured marriage, this one against the backdrop of the political corruption of Tammany Hall. A day's worth of work means something different to each of the Hallorans. To the bitter Mrs. Halloran, who looks "like a suffering saint," it is being reduced to ironing other people's clothes. To Mr. Halloran, who was let go after many years in a steady job at a grocery store, it means avoiding work and figuring out how to get his daily beer. The Hallorans are like many of Porter's poor whites in other parts of the country in that they are concerned with appearances. Like many characters throughout her canon, they live by illusions that make reality bearable. Mr. Halloran asks McCorkery for a political job, to which request McCorkery responds with "Ah, sure, sure . . . in a loud hearty voice with a kind of curse in it" (402). Halloran blends that with a memory/daydream in which McCorkery had said, "I've got a job for you up to your abilities at last; . . . name your figure in the way of money. And come up to the house sometimes . . . " (398). Halloran deceives himself sufficiently to tell his wife that he has a job in the McCorkery Club, a job that Mrs. Halloran knows is shady and had previously rejected, having held herself above the McCorkerys in the past. Nevertheless, she is able to create a false facade of respectability, as she tells their daughter, Maggie, "Yes, it's political work, toward the election time, with Gerald McCorkery. But that's no harm, getting votes and all, he'll be in the open air and it doesn't mean I'll have to associate with low people, now or ever. It's clean enough work, with good pay; if it's not just what I prayed for, still it beats nothing, Maggie. After all my trying . . . it's like a miracle" (406).

"A Day's Work" is rich in social commentary and psychological probing of the effect economic change has on a marriage with a fissure already present in its structure. The attraction Mr. Halloran has toward corrupt power and the repulsion Mrs. Halloran feels toward it identify their different class values. Although part of Mr. Halloran wants Connolly to escape the G-men who are after him for the numbers racket, an identification with the fellow Irish who are outsmarting the anti-Irish establishment, another part of him enjoys telling his wife that a man she had always admired for being a good Catholic is corrupt. The ambiguity of truth and the subjectivity of standards are reflected in the young

NEW ENGLAND AND GREENWICH VILLAGE

police officer O'Fallon, sworn to uphold the law, asking about Connolly, "What's the harm, I'd like to know? A man must get his money from somewhere when he's in politics. They oughta give him a chance" (395). In this story Porter's social satire is equal to that of "He," "Noon Wine," and "The Cracked Looking-Glass."

Notes

1. Harry J. Mooney, Jr., *The Fiction and Criticism of Katherine Anne Porter* (Pittsburgh: University of Pittsburgh Press, 1962) 47.

2. *The Collected Essays* 182–86.

3. William L. Nance, *Katherine Anne Porter and the Art of Rejection* (Chapel Hill: University of North Carolina Press, 1964) 17.

4. Nance 17.

5. George Hendrick, *Katherine Anne Porter* (New York: Twayne, 1965) 96.

6. Joan Givner, *Katherine Anne Porter: A Life* (New York: Simon and Schuster, 1982) 173.

7. Jane DeMouy, *Katherine Anne Porter's Women: The Eye of Her Fiction* (Austin: University of Texas Press, 1983) 63–66.

8. DeMouy 67.

9. DeMouy 71.

10. John Edward Hardy, *Katherine Anne Porter* (New York: Frederick Ungar, 1973) 59.

11. DeMouy 63.

12. Givner 303.

CHAPTER SIX

The Wartime Landscape

The two world wars of the first half of the twentieth century affected Porter as they did other writers of her generation, and in two short novels and *Ship of Fools* she probed the wartime atmosphere as both psychological and moral states of existence. "Pale Horse, Pale Rider" is set in 1918 near the end of the first war; "The Leaning Tower" and *Ship of Fools* are set in the period between the wars. In recreating and analyzing the mood of modern war, Porter finds universal themes that rise above topical concerns.

Both "Pale Horse, Pale Rider" and "The Leaning Tower" are long stories about initiation. In "Pale Horse, Pale Rider" the initiate is Porter's autobiographical heroine Miranda. Her counterpart in "The Leaning Tower" is Charles Upton, one of the few male protagonists in Porter's fiction. Wartime, which provides the background in both stories, illuminates death, which both characters confront, Miranda absorbing and accepting it and Charles simply identifying it simultaneously within himself and within world civilization.

104

THE WARTIME LANDSCAPE

"Pale Horse, Pale Rider"

On the surface "Pale Horse, Pale Rider," published in the *Southern Review* in 1939, is a recounting in fiction of Porter's nearly fatal bout with influenza in the epidemic of 1918. The background of the story is the newspaper world of Denver, and a subplot centers on a star-crossed love affair between Miranda and a young soldier named Adam Barclay. On another level the story is about Miranda's continuing journey toward self-identity, another step in her acquisition of essential truth. The events in "Pale Horse, Pale Rider" take place six years after the funeral of Gabriel at the end of "Old Mortality" and delineate more than the opposition between the romantic and the real; here the dichotomy is life and death. Miranda's experience in Denver takes place before the epiphany of "The Grave." If "Pale Horse, Pale Rider" contained only these two strata of meanings, it would belong exclusively to the company of "The Old Order" and "Old Mortality." But there is a further layer of meaning, bound up in the theme of spiritual malaise that is tied directly to wartime, and thus "Pale Horse, Pale Rider" is aligned with "The Leaning Tower" and *Ship of Fools*, all of which constitute Porter's contemporary response to war.

"Pale Horse, Pale Rider" is written in a structured stream-of-consciousness form with Porter guiding the reader through Miranda's dreams and describing the action that holds the dreams together in a plot. The story falls into three parts, like a play, with the first part introducing Miranda and extending to her collapse from illness. The most panoramic of the units, it depicts Miranda as a social being, the scenes shifting from her room to the newspaper office to the theatre, the dance hall, and the streets of the city. The second part describes Miranda's night of delirium in the room of the boardinghouse, with Miranda and Adam in the forestage. The third section reveals Miranda alone in the hospital, with only minor characters in the background, and it ends with her reentry into the world.[1] Dispersed among the three units are five dreams, the interpretations of which are critical to understanding all the meanings of the story.

The dream, vision, or reverie is a particular form that Porter favored throughout her writing. In her introduction to Eudora Welty's *A Curtain of Green* she admits to a "deeply personal preference" for the kind of story in which "external act and the internal voiceless life of the human imagination almost meet and mingle on the mysterious threshold between dream and waking, one reality refusing to admit or confirm the existence of the other, yet both conspiring toward the same end."[2] "Pale Horse, Pale Rider" is such a story. It is a combination of the waking life of Miranda and the sleeping reality in which truth is revealed to her in ways it could not otherwise be revealed.

The opening dream, the only one in the first section, sets into motion the most important symbols and establishes the ironic pattern and the major themes of the story. It displays Miranda's early struggle to assert her identity within her family (a link to "Old Mortality"), her fear of engulfment by her family, and her emerging awareness of death. The color gray (or silver) is prominent, as the middle ground between black and white (symbolizing interchangeably life and death), in the name of Miranda's horse "Graylie," who is not afraid of bridges, in the color of the stranger's horse, and in the memory of her kitten. The stranger, who is Death, is vaguely familiar to Miranda ("I know this man if I could place him. He is no stranger to me" [270]), an acquaintanceship that is reminiscent of Porter's comment that "We are born knowing death."[3] A symbolic journey also is begun in this section, but Miranda "does not mean to take it" (her dying is premature at this point) and wakes before it is completed. She wakes to the word "war," which is also a gong of warning. The remainder of the long first section develops the ideas of death, war, and journey, as Miranda's waking world and her social context are described.

In the middle unit of the story, which focuses on Miranda and Adam in her boardinghouse room, there are two dreams, the second and third. In the second dream Miranda dreams of the Rockies wearing their perpetual snow, gray moss, buzzards, and a tall sailing ship with a gangplank weathered to blackness, all images of black, white, and gray that amplify the oppositions of life and death and their midpoint, which is neither and both. Behind the ship is a jungle (the opposite of the snowcapped mountains), "a writhing terribly alive and secret place of death, creeping with tangles of spotted serpents, rainbow-colored birds with malign eyes . . . " (299). She sees herself running down the gangplank and the slender ship spreading its wings and sailing away into the jungle. Miranda awakens from this dream to two words, "danger" and "war," and thus the second journey is incomplete also.

In the third dream Miranda floats into "a small green wood, an angry dangerous wood full of inhuman concealed voices singing sharply like the whine of arrows." This wood, a version of the jungle, may also be Dante's image of mortal life. Within this wood, Adam, who has not appeared in the first two dreams, is twice seen falling from a flight of arrows but rising unwounded and alive both times. Only when Miranda interposes herself between Adam and the arrow does he die, an image that foreshadows Adam's death and expresses Miranda's guilt in exposing Adam to her contagious illness. Green is the only color image in this dream, but the reader recalls that the stranger, Death, in the first dream is "greenish."

The fourth and fifth dreams appear in the last section, in which Miranda is alone dying and then recovering, in the hospital. The dominating images are whiteness, silence, and cold, which Miranda in a nearly conscious moment associates with the absence of pain. A white fog, like that which moved into Granny Weatherall's consciousness, rises in Miranda's view. In it is concealed "all terror and all weariness, all the wrung faces and twisted backs and broken feet of abused, outraged living things, all the shapes of their confused pain and their estranged hearts" (308), images and ideas that are the sum of mortal life. She thinks of the German doctor, Dr. Hildesheim, who is treating her, as the enemy—the "Boche"—his face a skull beneath his helmet as he comes across the field with a naked infant writhing on the point of his bayonet and a huge stone pot marked "Poison." He throws the child and the poison into a well on Miranda's father's farm and contaminates its pure water with death as he symbolically returns the child, Miranda's surrogate, to the womb. The dream suggests that Miranda's childhood innocence has been poisoned by the war, and it also illustrates the degree to which wartime hysteria and racism, exhibited in the first unit, have invaded Miranda's private world, in which death and war have mingled. In this dream while her conscious mind is still grasping at logic, she thinks, "The road to death is a long march beset with all evils," an image associated with the journey metaphor but also associated with the war song "There's a Long, Long Trail," mentioned several times in the story. These interwoven references, amplified by the three funeral processions Miranda and Adam observe, point to war as a metaphor for the state of mortal existence, which is a continuous journey to death.

After the fourth dream, Miranda's mind splits into two parts, one reasoning and one frenzied. The split continues in the fifth and last dream, the longest and most complex, as Miranda, still clinging to mortality but close to death, tries to contemplate oblivion but still relies on images of things to grasp the idea. She thinks of it as a whirlpool of gray water and of herself lying on a granite ledge over a pit that she knows is bottomless. She resists the idea of nothingness at first but then acknowledges that there are finally no things that are the equivalent of death. As she begins to understand nothingness and to accommodate herself to it, "all notions of the mind, the reasonable inquiries of doubt, all ties of blood and the desires of the heart," dissolve and fall away until all that is left is "a minute fiercely burning particle of being that knew itself alone" and that was "composed entirely of one single motive, the stubborn will to live" (310–11). This particle of being says "Trust me" and "I stay" and grows to a fine radiance that curves out into a rainbow through which Miranda sees Paradise. Without warning, however, in the midst of Miranda's ecstasy, in the company of all the living she had known, "pure identities," there is "a vague tremor of apprehension" because something or someone is missing. It is of course Adam, who Miranda thinks is still among the physically alive. Upon this thought a curtain falls, and Miranda is alone in a strange stony place reminiscent of the symbolic terrain of Dante's journey through hell and purgatory. Pain returns, and Miranda resumes her journey back to life and thereon to death. This dream ends, like the first and third dreams, on a note of war as screaming bells, shrill whistles, and exploding lights signal the Armistice.

A point of confusion in the last dream is the reversal of life and death, a paradox that points to the most important meaning of the story. When Miranda is approaching death, the prospect is terrible, a landscape of disaster. But the perspective is that of the physically alive person to whom death is abhorrent and whose physical being suffers the agonies of physical decay. Once in Paradise, however, the physical self and consequently the pain and fear left behind, Miranda rejoices in the land of the spiritually alive, of those who cast no shadows in a place where it is "always morning." The perspective now is that of the pure spirit to whom the physical life is the equivalent of death. The inversion explains Miranda's difficult adjustment to being physically alive again. She asks, "What has become of the sun?" and "Shall I ever see light again?" The human faces around her seem dull and tired with none of the radiance she remembers from her dream. Miranda looks around her "with the covertly hostile eyes of an alien who does not like the country in which he finds himself" (313). Life is the ultimate irony, and it is with extraordinary effort that Miranda, who is likened to Lazarus, takes up her journey again, symbolized by her gray suede gloves and her walking stick.

Miranda's illness is grounded in a real influenza epidemic, but because her illness is associated with the war (it ends with the Armistice), it symbolizes the spiritual malaise of the twentieth century that nurtured catastrophic world wars.[4] The title is from Revelations 6:8: "And I looked, and behold a pale horse: and his name that sat on him was Death, and Hell followed with him. And power was given unto them over the fourth part of the earth, to kill with sword, and with hunger, and with death, and with the beasts of the earth." It is an allegory of Miranda's mortal experience. Adam is in many ways Miranda's opposite, his masculinity opposed to her femininity, his innocence opposed to her cynicism. The Biblical significance of his name lies in his experience within the story. As the innocent (he is referred to as the lamb), he must be sacrificed on the altar of the modern century's awful knowledge.

"The Leaning Tower"

"The Leaning Tower" appeared in 1941, three years after "Pale Horse, Pale Rider," and it also was published in the *Southern Review*. Some of the characters and scenes of this short novel are based on Porter's own experience in Berlin, but by the time she set about writing the story in 1940 the original experience was viewed through the lens of the intervening years in which the fearful promise of Nazism was being fulfilled. The events in "The Leaning Tower" are confined to five days in Berlin, where Charles Upton, a young American artist is absorbing impressions about Germany and the society represented by the boardinghouse in which he lives. Charles's story is much like the stories of Laura in "Flowering Judas," the protagonists of "Theft" and "Holiday," and Miranda in "Old Mortality." Charles is traveling toward truth, but he arrives only halfway. At the end of his story, Charles's drunkenness produces

THE WARTIME LANDSCAPE

the kind of delirium that is similar to a dream, and in this state an elusive truth hovers about him. All that he clearly apprehends is an oppression, an uneasiness, a knowledge that he will never be the same again, and an unanswered question about the leaning tower, which has some kind of ungraspable meaning: "What had the silly little thing reminded him of before? There was an answer if he could think what it was, but this was not the time" (495). Like Miranda, he will have to wait until memory and time transform the adventure into experience.

The meaning of the leaning tower is central not only to Charles's reverie but also to the story itself, and it is too simplistic to see the plaster tower as the symbol for Nazi Germany, whose fragility will surely lead to its disintegration. The key to the little tower's meaning lies in its history, in the characters Charles encounters, and in its association with another symbol in the story. Rosa, the landlady, brought the small plaster replica of the Tower of Pisa from Italy as a souvenir of her Italian journey, "the three happiest months" of her life. For her it represents an ideal place and time to which she longs to return. All the other characters have cherished illusions. For Hans, the Heidelburg student with the ugly dueling scar, it is the romantic past of Germany, or Paris as a substitute; for Tadeuz Mey, a young cynical Polish pianist, it is London; for Otto Bussen, a starving mathematics student, it is death or a cabaret; for the barber it is Malaga; for Charles's father, it was Mexico, where the horses had silver bridles. For Charles himself it has been Berlin, an image created by his friend Kuno, who had said, "If you don't go to Berlin, you miss everything" and talked about the city in such a way that Charles "in his imagination saw it as a great shimmering city of castles towering in misty light" (439). Because of Kuno, Charles has come to Berlin naively expecting to find his ideal. Instead he sees starvation, misery, dullness, fanaticism, in fact everything opposite to his idealized vision. Soon after Charles agrees to stay at Rosa's, he feels "a blind resentment all the more deep because it could have no particular object, and helpless as if he had let himself be misled by bad advice." He identifies the bad advice subconsciously with Kuno: "Vaguely but in the most ghastly sort of way he felt that someone he trusted had left him in the lurch, and of course, that was nonsense, as Kuno used to say. 'Nonsense' was one of Kuno's favorite words" (454).

The plaster tower, which Charles accidentally breaks, represents all their illusions, including the ideal that Nazi Germany is for some who adulate the "little shouting politician, toplock on end, wide-stretched mouth adorned by a square mustache" (451). A dream Charles has links the house of Germany to the plaster tower. Charles dreams the house is burning down, and as he flees "the dark skeleton of the house," he sees it "tall as a tower standing in a fountain of fire." One of the themes of "The Leaning Tower" is the illusion of idealism and the great disparity between appearance and reality. Rosa, by mending the tower and replacing it in its former position of honor, indicates that for her the self-delusion was still thriving in 1931.

Another symbol in the story, a dozen infant-sized pottery cupids that adorn the roof of a house across the street from Charles's boardinghouse, also helps explain the leaning tower. Immediately after breaking the plaster tower, Charles draws the curtains back and through the winter light observes the cupids, "gross, squat limbed, wanton in posture and vulgarly pink, with scarlet feet and cheeks and backsides, engaged in what appeared to be a perpetual scramble to avoid falling off the steep roof. . . . " Charles grimly notes "their realistic toe holds among the slate, their clutching fat hands, their imbecile grins. In pouring rain," he thinks, "they must keep up their senseless play. In snow, their noses would be completely buried. Their behinds were natural victims to the winter winds. And to think that whoever had put them there had meant them to be oh, so whimsical and so amusing, year in, year out" (447). In the final paragraph of the story, when Charles is contemplating the mended tower and wondering about its meaning, he connects it with the cupids: "Leaning, suspended, perpetually ready to fall but never falling quite, the venturesome little object—a mistake in the first place, a whimsical pain in the neck, really, towers shouldn't lean in the first place; a curiosity, like those cupids falling off the roof—yet had some kind of meaning in Charles' mind" (495). He feels "something terribly urgent at work, in him or around him, . . .

something perishable but threatening, uneasy, hanging over his head or stirring angrily, dangerously, at his back" (495). The tower comes to symbolize death, as Charles subsequently feels "what he had never known before, an infernal isolation of spirit, the chill and the knowledge of death in him" (495). The plaster tower and the pottery cupids are dead ideas fixed in time, whimsical and inappropriate representations of art, just as the holiday festivities are inappropriate responses to the conditions of modern civilization. Four days before New Year's Charles thinks, "It would be a relief when the necessity for appearing to celebrate something was over" (441).

The structure of the story further illuminates the tower's meaning. Like "Pale Horse, Pale Rider," "The Leaning Tower" has a three-part structure. Porter indicates the nearly equal divisions with space breaks in the text. The first part, which begins in the cafe across the street from Charles's dull little hotel in Hedeman-strasse, includes his reminiscences of his family, Kuno, and his life in Texas; his impressions of Berlin society; his securing a room at Rosa's boarding house and breaking the plaster replica of the tower of Pisa; and his learning the names and identities of his fellow boarders. The section ends with Charles's admitting to feeling young, ignorant, and awkward and listening to one of the boarders playing Chopin. The second section begins with Charles's dreaming that he is in a towerlike burning house and ends with his meeting the twins who are opening a cabaret on New Year's Eve. The section develops his association with the boarders, who represent modern society. Porter uses space breaks every few pages in this middle part to define Charles's separate social experiences in the boarding house. The third section begins with the New Year's Eve celebration in the cabaret and ends with Charles's awareness of death. This last section builds upon the first two sections and clarifies the universal meaning of this story, which has been erroneously construed as only a statement about Germany. The camaraderie Charles felt for his fellow boarders in the second section is soon dispelled. They argue among themselves from nationalistic viewpoints over the superiority of their individual cultures and attack the French, the English, the Italians, and Americans. Charles tries to inject some common sense: "I can't talk about whole countries because I never knew one, not even my own. I only know a few persons here and there and some I like and some I don't like and I never thought it anything but a personal matter . . . " (483–84). Tadeuz Mey, the Polish piano student, interrupts him with a statement that though spoken sarcastically nevertheless explains international relations: "Oh, dear fellow, that is being much too modest. The whole art of self-importance is to raise your personal likes and dislikes to the plane of moral or aesthetic principle, and to apply on an international scale your smallest personal experience. . . . If someone steps on your foot, you should not rest until you have raised an army to avenge you . . . " (484). Charles begins to understand an important idea during the course of the ensuing protracted conversation about politics and race relations. He feels something "like the first symptom of some fatal sickness, . . . a most awful premonition of disaster," and his thoughts revolve "dimly around vague remembered tales of Napoleon and Genghis Khan and Attila the Hun and all the Caesars and Alexander the Great and Darius and the dim Pharaohs and the lost Babylon." He feels "helpless" and "undefended" (488). Charles senses that the present contention among nations is merely the most recent segment in an ancient continuum of wars. Porter's sentence, with the repetitive *ands*, conveys the unbroken line of historical conflict. Charles perceives the destructive will to power within the human race, and it is this impending death of another era of civilization he feels as much as the seed of death within himself. The meaning of the fragile and foolish plaster tower, treasured and protected by Rosa and all the people who live by illusions, is extended to include far more than an ideal or the German state. It represents civilization itself.

Throughout all three parts Porter uses images and symbols to create an atmosphere of death, the most notable of which are again whiteness, snow, and cold. She works into all sections reminders of the essential causes of battles. Although nationalistic or even regionalistic pride is presented as a major cause of enmity, she also underscores the powerful role of money in inciting wars. The inflation, poverty, and class disparity depicted in Berlin have led to greed, avarice, and cruelty, all human failings revealed in Porter's brilliant descriptions of the pig-worshipers, obese Berliners who gaze longingly at pork products and artificial pigs (443). Even Charles's financial security is a reason for others to hate him.

The final theme in the story is a subtle statement about art and the artist's role in society. The plaster tower and the pottery cupids fail to fulfill an aesthetic ideal, but allusions to other artists and musicians such as Holbein, Dürer, and Chopin establish a standard to which Charles can aspire. Early in the story Charles detaches himself from the suffering people he sees in the streets of Berlin in order to draw them. But later his artistic impulse serves another, more noble, purpose. As a way of purging his feelings of disgust and malice, he draws the people he has encountered in Berlin, the people at the hotel, the boarders, and Rosa, the landlady. What begins in hatred and revulsion grows into tenderness as he works, and through the exercise of his artistic craft Charles concludes that they are all "good people" who are merely in "terrible trouble." Porter implies that art has the potential to redeem humanity through love. At the end of the story, however, it seems clear that the potential will not be realized. And even Charles is unable to articulate what he has intuited about the human condition. Like Miranda in the early part of "The Grave," he must wait for full understanding. Porter's ironic point of view, the cynical perspective of the author's voice superimposed over the limited awareness of the protagonist, makes a larger insight possible for the reader.

Notes

1. See Sarah Youngblood, "Structure and Imagery in 'Pale Horse, Pale Rider,' " *Modern Fiction Studies* 5 (1959–60): 344–52.

2. *The Collected Essays* 289.

3. " 'Noon Wine': The Sources," *The Collected Essays* 474.

4. See Edward G. Schwartz, "The Fictions of Memory," *Southwest Review* 45 (1960): 204–15.

CHAPTER SEVEN

Ship of Fools

Porter wrote *Ship of Fools* piecemeal between 1931 and 1961, seriously setting about unifying the parts and completing the work in 1960. Its publication in 1962 marked the culmination of her fictional canon.

The critical response to Porter's long-awaited *magnum opus* was mixed, ranging from Mark Schorer's declaration that *Ship of Fools* should be ranked among "the greatest novels of the past hundred years"[1] to Theodore Solotaroff's charge that Porter, failing to present an allegory of "the ship of this world on its voyage to eternity," had instead provided a labored account of a tedious voyage that revealed to the reader "little more than misanthropy and clever technique."[2] The disparity among reviews and reader response can be accounted for in several ways. Although it was inevitable that such a long-awaited work would fail to fulfill, to some degree, the reading public's anticipation, some readers also were put off by what they saw as unfair depictions of groups, Solotaroff objecting to Porter's presentation of Herr Löwenthal as "the stage Jew of the modern literary tradition," and *Die Welt*'s reviewer labeling *Ship of Fools* a "Document of Hatred."[3] Still other readers had difficulty adjusting to the form of the work. Wayne Booth admitted that *Ship of Fools* fell afoul of his own bias for finely constructed concentrated plots and complained that Porter's manner of narration was "fragmented," that her method was "sporadic," and that her unity was "based on theme and idea rather than coherence of action."[4] While these responses caused Porter to declare that not one reviewer had really understood her work, such responses can help the reader more fruitfully approach *Ship of Fools*.

Reading *Ship of Fools* as a novel requires that readers expand their understanding of the term *novel*. M. M. Liberman argues persuasively that the work is more properly an apologue or a beast epic, a series of connected satiric tales acted out by animal characters. Thus he says, Porter's "employment of modern short story strategies was not only appropriate but indispensable." By its nature, Liberman contends in response to Booth, *Ship of Fools* is in fact required to "have a large cast, to be fragmented in its narration, . . . to achieve unity based on theme and idea rather than coherence of action," and "to have no steady center of interest except the progressively more intense exemplification of its central truth."[5] Smith Kirkpatrick reinforces Liberman's position by explaining that there is "no clearly identifiable protagonist or antagonist in *Ship of Fools* because Porter's subject is too large to be shown through a central character."[6] By relinquishing the expectation that *Ship of Fools* will read like a traditional novel, readers are free to consider exactly what *Ship of Fools* is and what Porter's predisposition was. If all the shorter fiction and *Ship of Fools* are considered together, Porter's principal subject emerges as the journey toward truth, and *Ship of Fools* can be seen not only as the externalization of the journey metaphor that was implicit in the earlier works but also the encompassment of the characters and motifs developed in the preceding stories. There is finally no question that *Ship of Fools* is a rich and complex work, or that Porter intended it to be. She described it as the sum of what she knew about human nature. She also insisted that there was goodness in the microcosmic world she created and that she herself was a passenger on the ship.[7]

The surface experience of *Ship of Fools* was provided by Porter's own voyage from Veracruz to Bremerhaven in 1931. In a prefatory note to the novel she also said that *Ship of Fools* was inspired by Sebastian Brant's fifteenth-century moral allegory *Das Narrenschiff*, which she read in 1934 and which provided both the title and the central image for her own novel. Robert N. Hertz has carefully plotted the similarities and differences in the two works, underscoring his study with the contention that "*Ship of Fools* is plainly not a conventional fictional narrative" and "does not lend itself unprotestingly to familiar critical descriptions and proscriptions." He in turn describes *Ship of Fools* as "a kind of aquatic *Pilgrim's Progress"* with Porter "no less comprehensive or scrupulous in her vision and presentation of man's plight and potential salvation than, for example, were Bunyan or Brant or Milton." Hertz goes on to say that although *Ship of Fools* is substantially different from *Das Narrenschiff* in fundamental ways, among which is Brant's relentless defense of Christian ethics and theology, *Ship of Fools* exposes the same universality of folly as does Brant's work, "with only the self-righteous admonitions . . . missing."[8]

Even though its structure is unconventional, *Ship of Fools* does have form. It is divided neatly into three parts, each one distinguished by a title and an epigraph. Part I, "Embarkation," is identified with a line from Baudelaire which translates "When shall we set out toward happiness?" Part II, "High Sea," is explained by the title of a Brahms song, "Kein Haus, Keine Heimat" (No House, No Homeland), and Part III, "The Harbors," is completed with a quotation from Saint Paul, "For here have we no continuing city." It is a mistake to see the three parts as the equivalent of a dramatic structure. They represent only three stages of the voyage rather than the points in the rising and falling action of a plot. Porter explained the structure of her novel as "the movement of the ship, forward, the movement of the waves, the movement of the passengers as they walk about the decks, all these got into the structure of the book. It moves in all these ways."[9] The epigraphs appended to the section titles point to the primary subject of the novel, the search for happiness and the inevitable disillusionment that follows. If the voyage of the ship of fools is symbolic of the voyage of life, the single most significant trait of these voyagers is their capacity for clinging to illusions. When they embark, they are beginning a quest, looking for a place that ensures happiness, as the quotation from Baudelaire suggests. When they are on the high sea, they are in the middle of a journey without the security of land, not yet arrived at their destination. In the final part, the arrival at the destination port, home for many of the passengers, is clearly not the arrival at happiness, or at eternity as the Biblical quotation implies, or at eternal truth, as Porter's design proposes. Those who mistake home for truth, or the journey's end for fulfillment, have neither the hindsight of historical perspective nor the superior viewpoint shared by the author and the reader. The passengers act out Porter's themes as their stories unfold in segments from an omniscient point of view that focuses on one character or group of characters at a time, creating in its effect a multiplicity of viewpoints that captures the richness of a microcosmic society and establishes an overview of reality.

The themes that dominate this novel are multiple and interrelated. The illusions which people create and live by are explored in particular ways, but the grand illusion that guides the ship is that they are all going forward to something better. The reality is that they are going forward to something worse than their wildest imaginings. In this pell-mell race to the future, the voyagers are isolated from one another in, for the most part, loveless existences. They mistake or substitute lust, orderliness, or zeal for love, which Porter shows to be the mystery of life capable of uniting all people. She also takes up the question of evil, its sources and its nourishment in contemporary society. Porter's philosophical position, however, is not that of the determinist. The foolish voyagers are not simply condemned to be fools; they have free will, and the opportunities to see truth clearly exist all around them. Indeed, they are being carried by "truth" (the *Vera*) but are too blind to see it. Porter's pragmatic realism is sustained throughout the novel, and the passengers gain enough insights to prove her point.

The narrative is framed by the ports of Veracruz and Bremerhaven, but much more is seen of Veracruz because the themes and characters are introduced in that Mexican port town before the voyage gets underway. In fact, a careful examination of the opening frame can provide the reader with a thematic key for the rest of the novel. The relationship between the name Veracruz (true cross) and the name of the ship the *Vera* underscores the relationship between the port society and the ship's society. Porter describes first the port town of Veracruz and then representative Veracruzanos. She depicts the town as a typical, seedy port town, and the natives as self-satisfied, bigoted, cruel, and exploitive. She also presents a monkey, parrot, and dog, setting up a parallel with the humans and giving point to the animal images throughout the novel. The passengers that pass through the town to board the ship are described

SHIP OF FOOLS

in caricature without names. The passengers are thought of as sheep or swine by the Veracruzanos, who treat their own no better, but the narrative voice calls the passengers "birds of passage" and introduces a leggy girl "screaming like a peahen," a "pink and pig-snouted man," a child whose mother has made "a monkey" of him by dressing him in leather in August, a young woman who is called a "mule" by a Mexican clerk, and four pretty Spanish girls who are "noisy as a flock of quarreling birds." Also introduced are a fat man and woman and their fat white bulldog, four slim young men who accompany the Spanish girls, children who are twins, a pretty middle-aged woman who is pinched by a beggar, a young American girl with a young man in a white linen suit, and a gaunt blond man with huge hands and feet. The fact that no names are provided suggests that an absence of identity is their common condition. The narrator describes them collectively: "Imperfectly washed, untidy and dusty, vaguely not-present in eyes dark-circled by fatigue and anxiety, each one carried signed, stamped papers as proof that he had been born in a certain time and place, had a name of his own, a foothold of some kind in this world, a journey in view for good and sufficient reasons, and possessions worth looking into at international frontiers" (9).[10]

The passengers are connected in their anonymity and ignorance, and they also share a common illusion and a common predicament. Porter makes the point explicity: "So far they were all alike, and they shared a common hope. They lived individually and in mass for the sole purpose of getting safely that same day on board a German ship then standing in dock. . . . All believed they were bound for a place for some reason more desirable than the place they were leaving" (9–10). Instead of their shared suffering drawing them together, however, each passenger chooses "to maintain his pride and separateness within himself. . . . No bond was established between them" (11).

The first name the reader learns is that of the dog Bébé, but the first person who is introduced by name is Dr. Schumann, and he thus stands apart from the nameless passengers. He is also described in positive terms, without the cynicism of the earlier narrative voice. It is from his perspective that nameless passengers are further described, some for the first time: a hunchback, a tall sulky boy pushing a man in a wheelchair, a young Mexican mother with her Indian nurse, a family of colorless parents with an oversized daughter, two Mexican priests, a small German woman in black, a German Jew carrying a heavy sample case, an inhumanly fat Mexican man in a cherry-colored cotton shirt, and at the last moment, a bride and groom. The descriptions unfold against a background of "light-haired, very young, rather undersized ship's officers in white, and a crew of big solid blunt-faced sailors moving about their duties."

When the ship glides out of the harbor, each of the passengers discovers again what it was he had believed lost for a while, his identity. "Bit by bit it emerged, travel-worn, halfhearted but still breathing, from a piece of luggage or some familiar possession in which he had once invested his pride of ownership" (21). And here their identities are gradually revealed: The peahen is Lizzi Spökenkieker, the man with large hands and feet is Arne Hansen, the pig-snouted man is Herr Rieber, the young man in the white linen suit is David Scott, the hunchback is Herr Glocken, the young American girl is Jenny Brown, the middle-aged American woman is Mrs. Treadwell, the German woman in black is Frau Otto Schmitt, recently widowed; the family with the little boy in the leather suit is Herr and Frau Baumgartner and Hans. The reader meets Frau Rittersdorf, the Huttens with the bulldog Bébé, the Lutzes with the large daughter, Elsa, William Denny, William Freytag, Señora Esperón y Chavez de Ortega with her child and her Indian maid, Nicolasa, and the Jewish salesman Herr Löwenthal. Before Part I ends, the names of the Spanish dancers are revealed, and a group of Cuban students is presented. Early in Part II, the names of the twins are given, Ric and Rac, as are those of the boy Johann and his dying uncle Herr Graf, two Mexican priests Father Garza and Father Carillo, and the remainder of the Spanish dance troupe. Captain Thiele is introduced, and La Condesa makes her entrance. The name of the woodcarver who sacrifices himself to save Bébé is given only after his death in the long middle section. The reader is not given the names of the bride and groom, or the political agitator. They represent ideas exclusively and are not humanized in the narrative. Porter's weaving viewpoint reveals background stories and the major episodes: Jenny's facing the truth of her relationship to David, the ostracism of Freytag, the coup of the Zarzuela dancers, Etchegaray's giving his life to rescue a dog, the beating of Denny by Mrs. Treadwell, and the crisis in the love affair of Dr. Schumann and La Condesa. Juxtaposing comic relief to the main events is the pursuit of Lizzi Spökenkieker by Herr Rieber.

Representing various nations, the passengers and crew exhibit chauvinistic and racist attitudes. Because the *Vera* is a German ship and destined ultimately for Bremerhaven, the crew and the greatest number of first-class passengers are German. Liberman, among others, has observed that Porter, who was criticized for her depiction of Germans in "The Leaning Tower" as well as *Ship of Fools*, saw the Germans as "representations rather than presentations. . . . less persons than fictionalized figures and types."[11] All the Germans exhibit a sentimental pride in the fatherland, but beyond that they divide into two groups, those who value the old Germany and those who value the new Germany, the former "romantic" and "soft-headed," and the latter "new," "tough," and "strong."[12] Dr. Schumann, sporting a "beauty" of a dueling scar and bearing the name of a German romantic musician, represents the old Germany. In contrast, Captain Thiele is the most visible representative of the new Germany, although he holds a certain idealized view of the past and prefers the company of Schumann to that of the other Germans on board. He thinks of the very spirit of civilization as "that great Germanic force of life in which . . . Science and Philosophy moved hand in hand ruled by Christianity" (216). He has a firm sense of an ordered universe and his own obligation to preserve the order. "As Captain," he thinks, "he belonged to a larger plan, he fulfilled his destiny in his appointed place as representative of the higher law; if he failed in his duty—and the very foundation of his duty was to exact implicit obedience from every soul on the ship, without exception—why, then the whole structure of society founded on Divine Law would be weakened by so much" (174). His structure is hierarchical, with "human refuse," such as the passengers in the steerage, on the lowest rung, women lower than men, himself and others at the positions of power. "To put people in their proper places and keep them there cannot be called severity, nor defense. It is merely observing and carrying out the natural order of things" (248). It is this mentality that fosters such excesses as Nazism, the notion of a master Aryan race untainted by other races, the anti-semitism expressed by Lizzi Spökenkieker and Herr Rieber, among others, and euthanasia for defective children which Frau Rittersdorf proposes in her journal.

Nationalism is depicted also in the Texan William Denny, who makes both the pride and the disdain regional and ethnic. He prefers his native Brownsville because there "a man knew who was who and who was what, and niggers, crazy Swedes, Jews, greasers, boneheaded Micks, polacks, wops, Guineas and damn Yankees knew their place and stayed in it" (33–34). The narrow view of the supremacy of one's own group lies behind paternalism and sexism, Porter shows, as she continues to explore these forces that were treated thematically in the Mexican stories and the Miranda cycle.

Women as a class illustrate important ideas in *Ship of Fools*. With the exception of Jenny Brown, not one has an individual identity. All are subordinate to a male authority, as the use of titles sometimes indicates. Frau Hutten bows to her husband's primary position, as do Frau Baumgartner and Frau Lutz. Señora Ortega holds herself in fealty to her absent husband, and Frau Rittersdorf and Frau Otto Schmitt have each idealized their dead husbands. The female members of the Zarzuela troupe are controlled by their male counterparts, who procure customers for them and whip them into line. The necessity for the female to assert herself is an old theme in Porter's fiction. Through her art Jenny Brown was able to break the ties of her family and to begin establishing a separate identity.

Other characters, in varying degrees of fullness, caricature other ideas. Frau Rittersdorf represents, in addition to Nazism and husband-worship, the aspect of the artist that is the eavesdropper, the exposer. It is she who records in her notebook bits of unflattering information about the other passengers, and it is this same kind of information that the Zarzuela dancers post as notices on the ship's bulletin board as a form of blackmail. Jenny Brown, who draws caricatures of her fellow passengers, also is guilty of this invasion of privacy, which Porter abhorred even though, like Hawthorne, she recognized it as a necessary evil for the artist. The end to which the prying is put marks the difference. The artist, presumably, has noble goals to which he or she bends art.

Jenny Brown is more Porter's autobiographical center in the novel than any other single character, and her revealed past is similar in many ways to Porter's and likewise to Miranda's fictional experience. She is the developing young artist seeking her identity both as woman and artist, seeking love but holding out for real love, which she intuitively knows is different from what has bound her and David Scott together and fuels her attraction to Wilhelm Freytag. During the course of the voyage she gains insights and makes progress toward truth like her canonical sister Miranda. Mrs. Treadwell may very well represent another facet of Porter's self experience. Older than Jenny Brown, she is proper and decorous, carrying with her illusions of a perfect place and suppressing an animal sexuality. When her violence erupts, William Denny is the victim.

According to Porter's notes made during the voyage that provided the inspiration for *Ship of Fools*, the Cuban exile who was the model for La Condesa was insane.[13] Porter describes her as a mad-woman, and as such her insanity contributes to the idea of the reasonless base of human love. Her love for Dr. Schumann is inexplicable as is his love for her, which moreover defies all the principles of his profession and religion.

The varied meanings of other characters help create

the wide range of the microcosmic world. Herr Graff is the religious fanatic who has lost his humanity. Johann, his nephew and caretaker, viewed by Dr. Schumann in "his preposterous cruel innocence," feels the burden of guilt his uncle lays upon him. Herr Glocken represents the physically deformed person whose will has been stunted. He tells David Scott, "You will not have to die in despair because you never had courage to live! You have taken hold of your own life, for that no man can ever make you sorry!" (276). Herr Baumgartner is the alcoholic and the perennial child who has failed to assume the social roles of father and husband.

David Scott, Jenny Brown's companion and sometimes lover, represents in Porter's philosophy the person who is spiritually dead. He is "cold" and "nearsighted" (sometimes "blind"), and he looks at the world mechanically. His face is "like a wax face with blue marble eyes" (388). His apathy (illustrated when he tells Jenny, "I give you up. I won't fight with you any longer. It's not worth it.") is reminiscent of Eddie's resignation in "Theft." His continual hunger is "in his bones, in his soul" (148), and Jenny even traces the causes of his spiritual impoverishment to a lack of love in his childhood, a theme that Porter treated in "The Downward Path to Wisdom" and explored in several essays. He shares such a loveless past with Mrs. Treadwell and Captain Thiele, as Porter points out the dangers of the absence of love.

Wilhelm Freytag shares some traits with David Scott, just as he shares with him Jenny's attention. Freytag is associated with images of blindness and cold, and the reader can infer that he, too, is spiritually dead. But here Freytag's story departs from David Scott's. He is ostracized by the other Germans because he has a Jewish wife, and much of his background story illustrates the extent to which he has avoided reality by self-delusion. Mrs. Treadwell thinks of him as "a born scene-maker," hinting at his creation of facade. But although he is persecuted because of his wife, his suffering takes on larger, symbolic overtones. He is the twentieth-century Christian man who is ambivalent toward his Judeo heritage. He both loves and hates Jews, loving his wife (or an idea of her) but abhorring Herr Löwenthal, to whose company he is relegated.

Herr Löwenthal is an unsympathetic character who allows Porter to avoid sentimentalizing the abuses of Nazism. He sells religious relics to Christians and is self-righteous in his religion, which he considers the only true religion. He represents religious intolerance, just as he is the victim of intolerance. But he is not the lone representative of religious bias. The Lutherans dislike Catholics and Jews. Denny, like Löwenthal, thinks Catholics look like heathens; the Catholics are intolerant of non-Catholics, and so on. Arne Hansen simply is intolerant of any belief in God, exclaiming, "Oh, what a foulness is religion!" (332). Only Dr. Schumann, a Catholic, represents a truly good religious person who is tolerant of others' beliefs.

Religion is often related to politics in Porter's fiction. The fat man in the cherry-colored shirt (probably representing communism) is disdainful of Catholicism because he associates the church with the abuse of peasants and Indians in Mexico. But he himself is abusive and despicable. Porter in fact contends that evil expressed as hate, cruelty, and malice, often is committed in the name of religion.

But evil is generated in other ways, too, and Porter considers evil from a variety of perspectives. In her depiction of the Zarzuela troupe and the twins Ric and Rac, Porter at first appears to be suggesting that evil is metaphysical. Ric and Rac, ironically christened Armando and Dolores (love and pity), seem to be demon-possessed, and they are thought to be "outside the human race" (330) by the other passengers. But Porter demolishes any such notion as she traces the cause of the twins' "evil" to the failure of their parents to love them. Part II ends with a horrifying depiction of Tito's torturing the twins because they have invaded the territory of the parent thieves. One of the most important thematic statements in *Ship of Fools* is what Porter called the "collusion in evil"[14] or the assistance of evil by apathy. Dr. Schumann explains the philosophy, which proposes that evil already exists in the human soul, waiting to be tapped: "Our collusion with evil is only negative, consent by default, you might say. I suppose in our hearts our sympathies are with the criminal because he really commits the deeds we only dream of doing! Imagine if the human race were really divided into embattled angels and invading devils—no, it is bad enough as it is—with nine-tenths of us half asleep and refusing to be waked up" (294).

If lack of love accounts for the evil nature of Ric and Rac, it also accounts for the Captain's inhumanity, Mrs. Treadwell's incompleteness, and the various kinds of unfulfillment other characters represent. And yet love is the most important idea in the novel. It is what each person wants and seems unable to find, or in the case of Dr. Schumann and La Condesa, to accept when they find it. Near the end of the voyage Mrs. Treadwell has a momentary insight, which is one of the most important thematic statements in the novel: "What they were saying to each other was only *Love me, love me in spite of all! Whether or not I love you, whether I am fit to love, whether you are able to love, even if there is no such thing as love, love me!*" (480). The awareness does not remain, however, because "a small deep wandering sensation of disgust, self-distaste," comes with her straying thoughts. But the great difficulty of making a loving connection is illustrated in the lack of success of the amorous pursuits on board the *Vera*: Freytag and Jenny, Freytag and Mrs. Treadwell, Jenny and David, Mrs. Treadwell and the purser, Elsa and the medical student, Denny and Ampara, Johann and the dancer, Hansen and the dancer, Dr. Schumann and La Condesa, and all the failed marriages represented in the pairs on board. Only the bride and groom have found true love, but even it is cursed with self-delusion because they believe they are immortal.

The central idea of self-delusion is supported throughout the novel by the dominant motif of the mask, which Kirkpatrick has explored.[15] Porter shows both the simple masks donned for the simplest of reasons and the intricately contrived masks that serve equally complex motives. Each passenger symbolically wears a mask that may represent nationality, philosophy, age, religion, social status, wealth, politics, morality, and what Kirkpatrick calls "all the other existential distinctions made by both the elemental and civilized man."[16] The masks may change, however, according to the audience, the occasion, or the time. The masks of love that "Jenny angel" and "David darling" wear hide the hate that coexists with the love, and by the same token the masks of hate routinely give way to those of love. Mary Champagne's name is a mask that hides her Jewish heritage. Herr Baumgartner's childish merrymaking is a mask for his unsettled account "with the female viper" (455). Herr Professor Hutten's academic rationalism is a mask for his inhumanity, in the way that many characters hide their malice and intolerance behind a mask of religion. Two characters who exhibit the mask motif in the most explicit way are Mrs. Treadwell, whose impeccable propriety hides the savagery she has suppressed, and William Denny, who chauvinistically identifies all the others by the masks he sees. Mrs. Treadwell thinks of her age as "a garment she could put off at will, a mask painted on her face" (414), and although she intends to pass up the masked ball, she amuses herself by painting on her face a mask "of unsurpassed savagery and sensuality." It is this mask that causes the drunken Denny, mistaking her for Pastora, to attack her in a frenzy of lust. When he is unconscious she beats him in furious pleasure with a high-heeled shoe, thus fulfilling the primitive savagery depicted by the mask. The motif culminates in the masked ball organized by the Zarzuela dancers to disguise their thievery. The mask motif is linked to the theme of appearance versus reality and also to Porter's contention that the discovery of truth is obscured by illusion.

Some characters are less heavily masked than others, and at least one is guileless. Etchegaray, the primitive woodcarver who rescues Bébé, acts out of an instinctual value for life. Both Jenny and Dr. Schumann are struggling to free themselves from self-delusion and from their vision-hampering masks. She makes progress in one direction, he another. She gradually is shedding the old restrictions of family and society, but she has not yet completed her identity or found true love. Dr. Schumann, on the other hand, knows who he is and is secure in that knowledge, but he cannot escape the constraints of his profession and his religion to accept the love of La Condesa.

The truth grasped by both Jenny and Dr. Schumann has been made available in part through dreams. Jenny's dream in which she sees her and David's relationship mirrored in the savagery of the Indian couple and Dr. Schumann's dream in which he faces his love for La Condesa provide momentary truths that will shape their lives. Captain Thiele's entertaining himself by dreaming about murdering from a position of authority defines Porter's fear about lawful evil, like that of Hatch in "Noon Wine." Nicolasa's dream about her mother further defines the importance of maternal love in the formation of the human soul. Jenny says of the voyage itself, "Soon it will be only a dream." David's response is true in a way he cannot see, as he says, "Dreams are real, too" (496).

At the end of the voyage, the remaining passengers on the *Vera* disembark at Bremerhaven, the broken haven, with their illusions and their isolation preserved. As the passengers line up at the gangplank, "eye met eyes again vaguely, almost without recognition and no further speech. They were becoming strangers again . . . [with] a pleasant indifference to everything but the blessed moment of escape to life once more" (494). Most have learned nothing during a voyage that should have reminded them metaphorically of the voyage of this world on its journey to eternity. The final scenes depict the renewed illusion, particularly the "illusion of joy," as all the German passengers, "mysteriously entranced as if they approached a lighted altar," prepare "to set their feet once more upon the holy earth of their Fatherland" (494); and as a young boy, "who looked as if he had never had enough to eat in his life, nor a kind word from anybody," stares with blinded eyes and whispers the German greeting "Grüss Gott, Grüss Gott" to the town, as if it were "a human being, a good and dear trusted friend who had come a long way to welcome him" (497).

The conclusion is particularly chilling because the reader is left to write the epilogue and to define precisely the extent of the illusion. The illusion, however, does not stop with the German idealization of the homeland because Porter makes clear that the contemporary voyage is simply a symbol for the journey of all humanity through life. It is the same voyage that Brant, Bunyan, Homer, Dante, and Joyce depict, and Porter has drawn inspiration and prototype from all of them as well as from her own experience in the twentieth century.

Notes

1. Mark Schorer, "We're All on the Passenger List," *New York Times Book Review* 1 Apr. 1962: 1.

2. Theodore Solotaroff, " 'Ship of Fools' and the Critics," *Commentary* 34 (Oct. 1962): 277–86.

3. Herbert von Borch, " 'The Germans are still cruel, evil and fanatic'/Document of Hatred: K. A. Porter's 'Ship of Fools' " ["Die Deutschen sind allzumal grausam, bose und fanatisch'/Dokument des Hasses: K. A. Porter's 'Narrenschiff' "] *Die Welt* 9 June 1962.

4. Wayne Booth, "Yes, But Are They Really Novels," *Yale Review* 51.4 (Summer 1962): 632–34.

5. M. M. Liberman, "The Responsibility of the Novelist: The Critical Reception of *Ship of Fools*," *Criticism* 8 (1966): 377–88.

6. Smith Kirkpatrick, "*Ship of Fools*," *Sewanee Review* 71 (1963): 94–98.

7. See Roy Newquist, "An Interview with Katherine Anne Porter," *McCall's* 92 (Aug. 1965): 88.

8. Robert N. Hertz, "Sebastian Brant and Porter's *Ship of Fools,*" *The Midwest Quarterly* 6 (1965): 389–401.

9. Elizabeth Janeway, "For Katherine Anne Porter, *Ship of Fools* Was a Lively Twenty-Two Year Voyage," *New York Times Book Review* 1 Apr. 1962: 4–5.

10. *Ship of Fools* (New York: Atlantic, Little, Brown, 1962) 21. The text is the first edition, to which page numbers in parentheses hereafter refer.

11. *Katherine Anne Porter's Fiction* 36.

12. See "Notes on Writing," *The Collected Essays* 443.

13. Darlene Harbour Unrue, *Truth and Vision in Katherine Anne Porter's Fiction* (Athens: University of Georgia Press, 1985) 243, n. 44.

14. See James Ruoff and Del Smith, "Katherine Anne Porter on *Ship of Fools,*" *College English* 24 (1963): 396–97.

15. See Kirkpatrick.

16. Kirkpatrick 94–95.

CHAPTER EIGHT

The Essays and Occasional Writings

Katherine Anne Porter's nonfictional writings, her essays, poems, reviews, published letters, and transcribed speeches, offer the student another aspect of her graceful writing. In the forward to *The Days Before* (1952) Porter defined the relationship between her fiction and nonfiction. She wrote, "This book would seem to represent the other half of a double life: but not in truth. It is all one thing. The two ways of working helped and supported each other: I needed both." She expressed the hope "that the reader will find in this collection of papers written throughout my thirty years as published writer, the shape, direction, and connective tissue of a continuous, central interest and preoccupation of a lifetime" (vii).

The Days Before was the first collection of Porter's nonfiction to appear; in 1970 an expanded gathering, *The Collected Essays and Occasional Writings of Katherine*

Anne Porter, was published. Other nonfictional works include *Katherine Anne Porter's French Song-Book*, a translation from the French of some children's songs, *Outline of Mexican Popular Arts and Crafts* (a long essay on the history of the popular arts in Mexico), several children's stories and an adult fable she retold, many book reviews, an account of a day she spent with her niece Mary Alice, *A Christmas Story*, and *The Never-Ending Wrong*, her account of the Sacco and Vanzetti affair of the 1920s.

The Days Before contains twenty-nine pieces placed in the categories "Critical," "Personal and Particular," and "Mexican." *The Collected Essays and Occasional Writings* contains all of *The Days Before*, additions in the three original categories, and new sections labeled "Biographical," "Cotton Mather," "On Writing," and "Poems." Except for the poetry, the classification often is arbitrary. Porter herself had difficulty placing the pieces, moving various works from *The Days Before* into different sections in *The Collected Essays*. With few exceptions the categories are interchangeable, for the boundaries blur as Porter weaves biography, criticism, personal experience, and social commentary into each piece. The pieces thus are a rich mine of fragments of Porter's worldview and her aesthetic theory, fragments which are interesting in their own right but can also be applied to a better understanding of her fiction.

Porter's critical judgments, wherever they appear, usually are unequivocal. In "On a Criticism of Thomas Hardy," first published in 1940, she summarizes her estimate of Hardy: "He practiced a stringent discipline, severely excised and eliminated all that seemed to him not useful or appropriate to his plan. In the end his work was the sum of his experience, he arrived at his particular true testimony; along the way, sometimes, many times, he wrote sublimely" (13). But the essay is more important for its contribution to an understanding of Porter's moral philosophy than it is for its assessment of Hardy. She takes as her departure points the Bishop of Wakefield's burning of *Jude the Obscure* and T. S. Eliot's charge that Hardy's fiction is unwholesome and unedifying. From there Porter launches a passionate attack on moralistic critics who confuse religion and art. She says, "Of all the evil emotions generated in the snake-pit of human nature, theological hatred is perhaps the most savage, being based on intellectual concepts disguised in the highest spiritual motives" (3–4). It is a stance that helps explain the religious biases in *Ship of Fools*, as does her statement in the essay that the mystical concept of God "has seemed at times not to know the difference between Good and Evil, but to get them hopelessly confused with legalistic right and wrong" (8). The issue of legality versus morality is also one of the central themes in "Noon Wine."

She attacks both theocracy and institutional religion (in other places she attacks other kinds of institutions), describing two kinds of people, the Believers and the Inquirers, and comes down on the side of the Inquirers, as she does throughout the fictional canon and notably in the Miranda stories, "Holiday," and "The Leaning

Tower." She makes clear in this essay that she is not an atheist, even if her idea of God is unorthodox: "Scientific experiment leads first to skepticism; but we have seen in our time, how, pursued to the verge of the infinite, it sometimes leads back again to a form of mysticism. There is at the heart of the universe a riddle no man can solve, and in the end, God may be the answer" (7).

"A Wreath for the Gamekeeper" (1960) begins with a two-pronged attack on censorship and writers or publishers who exploit the censorship issue for material profit. The title is an allusion to a scene in *Lady Chatterley's Lover* that Porter selects as particularly silly. The essay is a scathing attack on the novel as well as those critics who have praised it (including Archibald MacLeish, Edmund Wilson, Jacques Barzun, and Mark Schorer). It also is an attack on D. H. Lawrence, who was, according to Porter, a badly flawed artist.

The focus of her criticism is what she considers Lawrence's perversion of obscenity, romanticizing and mystifying simple animal nature. Porter, on the other hand, says that obscenity is "necessary as expression, a safety valve against the almost intolerable pressures and strains of relationships between men and women" (20). It is a position she assumes in "Holiday," when she depicts the hardworking German immigrant women who enjoy obscene jokes during a marriage celebration, and it is a position upon which she elaborates in a letter to her nephew Paul (109–110) and in another essay, "The

THE ESSAYS AND OCCASIONAL WRITINGS

Flower of Flowers." In "Marriage Is Belonging" she goes on to say, "Like all truly mystical things, love is rooted deeply and rightly in this world and in this flesh" (188). She agrees with Lawrence that the flesh is one of the many bridges to the spirit, but she disagrees with his making the flesh into a religion.

In the course of her argument against Lawrence, she also attacks Tolstoy (who "did not know the truth . . . about himself or about anyone else" [23]) and praises Yeats, as she does consistently throughout her nonfictional writing, citing him again and again as one of the significant influences on her development as an artist.[1] The statement she makes about Tolstoy and a particular one she makes about Lawrence are also pertinent to her fictional themes. In explaining Tolstoy's ignorance of human nature, she says that "all recorded human acts and words are open testimony to our endless efforts to know each other, and our failure to do so" (23), a statement that is at once a denial of a discernible spiritual connection celebrated by romantics and a delineation of the human compulsion to seek meaning through human connection. In disparaging Lawrence's views, she declares that he "admits unwillingly a fact you would think a sensible person would have been born knowing, or would have learned very early: that we *are* separate, each a unique entity, strangers by birth, that our envelopes are meant as the perfect device for keeping us separate" (26). It is a belief that has special bearing on *Ship of Fools*, which begins and ends with observations about the separateness of the ship's voyagers. In the novel Porter's irony is even more biting than it is in the essay.

"Reflections on Willa Cather" (1952) includes a brief account of Cather's life and contains little that is critically fresh about Cather's writing. But the essay does reveal some of Porter's more important critical and philosophical ideas and points to a significant psychological theory. She says that Gertrude Stein's *Tender Buttons* was the beginning of Porter's own quarrel with a certain school of modern writing "in which poverty of feeling and idea were disguised, but not well enough, in tricky techniques and disordered syntax (33), a not surprising statement in view of Porter's own clear style and profound themes. She praises Joyce's *Dubliners*, calling it "that small collection of matchless stories" which "was not a shock, but a revelation, a further unfolding of the deep world of the imagination" (33). She often cites Joyce as one of the world's great writers, and his influence on her is notable, especially in "The Cracked Looking-Glass" and "A Day's Work."[2] She also says in this essay, "I have not much interest in anyone's personal history after the tenth year, not even my own. Whatever one was going to be was all prepared for before that. The rest is merely confirmation, extension, development. Childhood is the fiery furnace in which we are melted down to essentials and that essential shaped for good" (31). Her view in this case is a restrained Freudianism, but Porter always stops short of absolute determinism. The shaping of essentials never precludes the capacity for knowing ourselves, but it produces good results only when it is combined with love. The absence of love is the horrifying fact in "The Downward Path to Wisdom" and "He," and it accounts for the malice of Ric and Rac in *Ship of Fools*, just as it explains the spiritual stagnation of David Scott, Mrs. Treadwell, and Captain Thiele.

The most important point Porter makes about Cather reveals still more about Porter's aesthetic. She observes that Cather did not take up newness for its own sake, that although she read the works of her contemporaries, she "held firmly to what she had found for herself" (38). Porter comments that "true art is provincial in the most realistic sense," obviously using the term "provincial" to refer not to the writer's relegation to a superficial regionalism but rather to the writer's most deeply rooted experience. For the conference on the Arts and Exchange of Persons in 1956 Porter had answered questions provided by the Institute of International Education about the exchange of writers aboard. One such question asked, "Is foreign experience valuable for the writer, or does it deprive him of his 'roots' "? Porter responded, "A human being carries his 'roots' in his blood, his nervous system[,] the brain cells; no man can get rid of them" ("Remarks on the Agenda" [220]).

"It is Hard to Stand in the Middle," an essay that takes its title from Ezra Pound's Canto XIII, is a review of Pound's letters of 1907–1941, collected and edited by D. D. Paige. Originally published as "Yours, Ezra

Pound" in 1950, the essay also is the longest of a series of statements Porter made about Pound, his influence on the twentieth century, and the issue of his treason. She considered him a supreme artist who put art above everything else. She said that all his letters related to "one sole theme—the arts" (41). In 1949 she wrote a letter to the editor of *The Saturday Review of Literature* in response to articles which had questioned the wisdom of awarding the Bollingen prize to Ezra Pound by the Society of Fellows of the Library of Congress in American Letters, of which Porter was a member. She defends the selection of Pound:

I am glad that he is being cared for, I pity his madness; the evil he has done is hateful to me, I reject it without reservation; but I remember the light that used to shine from his pages when he wrote about something he knew with his heart—poetry—and the beautiful translations, or paraphrases, from the Chinese and the Provençal, and how well he knew that art was not a marginal thing, but lived at the center of being by its own reality; that it was no decoration, but the Stone itself; no matter, he cannot commit treason against that, it is beyond the reach of his mortal part. (212)

Later, in a letter to her nephew Paul, she mentions "poor Ezra Pound, who was as good a poet as either [Frost or William Carlos Williams] and a critic who helped a whole generation of writers to find out what they were doing . . . " (119). In excerpts from her note-

THE ESSAYS AND OCCASIONAL WRITINGS

books that were first published in the *Southern Review* (1965), she pays Pound a significant compliment, reminiscent of an observation she made in "On a Criticism of Thomas Hardy" about the "untrained minds" which "have always been a nuisance to the military police of orthodoxy" (7). She says that she went to see Pound at St. Elizabeth's (a mental hospital in Washington, D.C.), where he was incarcerated after being charged with treason, and that she doubted then and still doubts "that Ezra Pound was ever for a moment insane. He was just a complete, natural phenomenon of Unreason" (300).

"Orpheus in Purgatory" (1950) is only superficially a review of *Rilke and Benvenuta*, by M. von Hattenberg. More specifically, it is about human love and the difficulty of finding it. Porter says, "It is hardly possible to exaggerate the lovelessness in which most people live, men or women: wanting love, unable to give it, or inspire it, unable to keep it if they get it, not knowing how to treat it, lacking the humility, or the very love itself that could teach them how to love: it is the painfullest thing in human life . . . " (53). It is a view that is imparted in much of Porter's fiction, appearing in "The Martyr," "Virgin Violeta," and the Miranda stories, and it anticipates Mrs. Treadwell's speech about love in *Ship of Fools*. In commenting about the women in Rilke's life, Porter suggests that all his women were seeking a "man-god" rather than the God in man, a theme she presents in "Flowering Judas," in the character of Mrs. Braggioni, and in "The Martyr."

"The Laughing Heat of the Sun" (1949) is a review of *The Canticle of the Rose*, a collection of more than thirty years of Edith Sitwell's work. Porter praises Sitwell's carefully wrought poetic designs and her use of symbolism, citing "The Song of the Cold" as a poem in which the symbol is particularly effective. She explains cold in this poem as "the symbol of poverty, death, and the hardened human heart," reminiscent of Porter's symbolic use of cold in "Pale Horse, Pale Rider" and looking ahead to the cold symbolism in *Ship of Fools*.

"On Christopher Sykes" (1951) is Porter's review of Sykes's *Character and Situation*, a collection of short stories introduced by Evelyn Waugh. Porter attacks both Sykes and Waugh, labeling them "the Romantic-Erotic-Religious" who "have a message to convey" (65). Her feminist ire is raised at what she regards as Sykes's "monkish distrust of women" which "leads him to set up some improbable figures of straw and wax, dressed in skirts, which he then slaps around so severely it becomes rather embarrassing to witness" (66).

Porter's essay on Virginia Woolf, originally published as "Virginia Woolf's Essays—A Great Art, A Sober Craft" in 1950, was occasioned by the appearance of *The Captain's Death Bed*, a collection of Virginia Woolf's essays edited by her husband, Leonard Woolf. Porter praises Virginia Woolf highly, saying she was "a great artist, one of the glories of our time" who "never published a line that was not worth reading" (70). And Porter reveals that Virginia Woolf was one of the writers

THE ESSAYS AND OCCASIONAL WRITINGS

who deeply "touched the real life" of Porter's own mind and feelings.

"On Modern Fiction," written in 1965, was Porter's contribution to a symposium on the subject of contemporary literary titans. She objects to the list sent her for ranking and wonders what the rationale was for leaving some names off and including others. Nevertheless she lists works by Warren, Tate, Welty, and Flannery O'Connor, among some others, as her choices, but insists upon acknowledging as well some older twentieth-century writers: E. M. Forster, Richard Hughes, Ford Madox Ford, Virginia Woolf, and James Joyce. She cites Hemingway's "Big Two-Hearted River" as especially meritorious. But Porter, who refused to be limited to twentieth-century currents, wants to press farther into the past and names *Moll Flanders* and the works of Austen, the Brontës, Dickens, Hardy, James, Hawthorne, Melville, and Twain. She warns against remembering the American past inaccurately and concludes, "If you look over this list, incomplete as it is, you will see that there is a line of march, unbroken and continuous and I believe due to go on for a good while. In spite of past, present, and future hell!" (88). It is a pertinent declaration in light of Porter's classical notions about style, truth, and models of art and separates her from many of her twentieth-century contemporaries.

"St. Augustine and the Bullfight" (1955) is a personal essay in which Porter identifies several concepts important to an understanding of much of her fiction. She distinguishes between *adventure* and *experience*, she points to the elusiveness of truth, and she describes the mission of the artist. She says that adventure is something a person seeks for pleasure or profit, and experience is "the truth that finally overtakes him," a contrast that helps explain the meaning of the conclusion to "The Grave," when Miranda transforms a memory into a timeless truth. Porter says that she often asks herself "What is truth," and she sees the purpose of the artist as that of shaping the chaos of the world into a semblance of order.

The heart of the essay is a personal experience she had at a Mexican bullfight, which she attended reluctantly but during which she discovered that she had a taste for blood, which she identifies as a part of human nature most people are reluctant to claim. It is a part of the human proclivity Miranda intuits in "The Circus." Porter's link to Saint Augustine is his story in the *Confessions* of a young friend who had been led into a similar kind of hateful "adventure" but had been strong enough to turn it into "experience." Throughout her canon Porter implies that the possibility for experience lies behind each adventure.

Porter was a prolific letter writer, but among personal letters to her family she chose to publish only two, both to her nephew Paul, one written in 1948 when he was a student at UCLA, and the other written in 1963. The first letter contains an analysis of love and an explanation of the two traditional schools of love, the "Foul Sex school" and the "True Love school." Porter adds a third, the "Stroke of Lightning school," in which

THE ESSAYS AND OCCASIONAL WRITINGS

an "Object becomes a Subject and is instantly transfigured with a light of such blinding brilliance all natural attributes disappear and are replaced by those usually associated with archangels at least" (111). Although those comments give definition to the theme of the deification of humans in "Virgin Violeta," "Flowering Judas," and "The Martyr," the letter is equally important for Porter's affirmation of her resistance to dogma. She refers to Fascism, Nazism, and Communism, saying, "I resist all three as you know" and describing the cross-purposes, confusion, and ambiguity in the three movements. In "A Letter to the Editor of *The Nation*" (May 11, 1947 [203]), she had called upon liberals to stop being used by either Communists or fascists, and in a report on a Town Meeting of the Air ("On Communism in Hollywood") she drew a comparison between this public assembly and Berlin of 1932, where political debaters were considered potential criminals.

The second letter to Paul (23 March 1963), who was afflicted with what he called "an obstinate depression of spirits," was written with the intention of cheering him. Porter describes the various interpretations of depression: medical (melancholy), psychological (inhibited libido), and theological (despair) and rounds out her letter with gossip and literary chitchat, mentioning her dislike of the works of Tennessee Williams, Becket, Jean Genet, Albee, and others, and expressing admiration for Yeats's one-act plays and for Molière's comedies.

Between 1955 and 1958 Porter reviewed two works

about Dylan Thomas and a collection of his letters to Vernon Watkins, all three of which she gathered for *The Collected Essays* under the title "Dylan Thomas." She admires Thomas' poetry and his hardworking approach to his craft but objects to the attempts to explain Thomas by his biographers, his friend John Malcolm Brinnin and his wife, Caitlin. Porter says, "No man can be explained by his personal history, least of all a poet," pointing out that the artistic vision is more than a sum of details and facts.

"A Defense of Circe" (1954) is a retelling of the Circe episode from *The Odyssey*. It follows the Butcher-Arnold translation and is reminiscent of Porter's apprenticeship days of retelling children's stories and fables. One of her best essays and the one that sheds the most light on her own fiction, it contains the same ironic tone as the fiction and illustrates one of her constant themes, the dark side of human nature that is denied by civilized men and women. She says of Circe, "Her unique power as goddess was that she could reveal to men the truth about themselves by showing to each man himself in his true shape according to his inmost nature. For this she was rightly dreaded and feared; her very name was a word of terror" (133). The essay also reveals Porter's ironic technique that, in this case, produces humor. The tone is not that of the naive innocent telling the story, like Twain's Huckleberry Finn, for example, or even the narrative voice in the Miranda stories, but rather it is that of the cynical, all-seeing narrator such as the narrative voice in *Ship of*

THE ESSAYS AND OCCASIONAL WRITINGS

Fools. Like the mock-epic, the essay trivializes the actions of both the immortals and the mortals and establishes *The Odyssey*, which Porter calls "the most enchanting thing ever dreamed of in the human imagination" (136), as one of her classical standards. Porter understands the Homeric world that is the context of the poem: "Odysseus was wise in his mortal wisdom: He knew that man cannot live as the gods do. His universal fate: birth, death, and the larger disasters, are from the gods; but within that circle he must work out his personal fate with or without their help" (139).

"The Flower of Flowers" (1950) is important for its explanation of Porter's understanding of rose symbolism, especially useful in interpreting "Flowering Judas." It also contains further statements on the relationship between the physical and the spiritual and on the distinction between religion and black magic, helpful in understanding "Magic" as well as "Flowering Judas." Porter says, "With very few exceptions among wild roses, they thrive best, any good gardener will tell you, in deep trenches bedded with aged cow manure" (148). It is a homely metaphor for the more exquisite point she makes in "The Grave" that out of death comes life, or out of a knowledge of death comes awareness of the life of the spirit, what Glenway Wescott has called the "tomb-womb" symbolism in Porter's art.[3] Porter says that "the rose is sacred to religion, to human love, and to the arts. It is associated with the longing for earthly joy, and for eternal life. There is a noticeable absence of them, or flowers of any kind in the textbooks of magic, witchcraft, the Black Arts by any name. The world of evil is mechanistic, furnished with alembics, retorts, ovens, grinding stones; herbs, mainly poisonous; the wheel but not the rose" (152–53). Her explanation gives definition to the evil world depicted in "Magic," and it gives the lie to the revolution, which idolizes the machine, in "Flowering Judas" and "Hacienda."

"Portrait: Old South" (1944) is an account of Porter's grandmother and grandfather and their wedding in Kentucky around 1850. She describes the legendary bridal table, representing the luxury and tradition of the Old South, and describes the family's later impoverishment by the Civil War that led to their migration to the Southwest. It is an important background piece for "The Old Order" and "Old Mortality."

"A House of My Own" (1941) is Porter's account of buying a modified Georgian farmhouse in upper New York state, of the feeling of "rightness" about the house. In her comments about the troubles of ownership, however, one sees the seeds for the relinquishing of the house thirteen months after the purchase and something of the same attitude she analyzed in the protagonist of "Theft."

"The Necessary Enemy" (1948) describes the symbiotic relationship of love and hate, both of which are natural to life and even nourish one another. "Hatred is part of it [love], the necessary enemy and ally," she says, and she describes a hypothetical young wife and husband who both love and hate one another. It is the conflict in "Rope," and the essay confirms that story's meaning. Porter attacks the concept of romantic love, which "crept into the marriage bed" and brought along "its absurd notions about love as eternal springtime and marriage as a personal adventure meant to provide personal happiness" (185). In this essay she makes one of her most profound statements about evil, which reflects a philosophical stance apparent in many of the stories and *Ship of Fools*:

The refusal to acknowledge the evils in ourselves which therefore are implicit in any human situation is as extreme and unworkable a proposition as the doctrine of total depravity; but somewhere between them, or maybe beyond them, there does exist a possibility for reconciliation between our desires for impossible satisfactions and the simple unalterable fact that we also desire to be unhappy and that we create our own sufferings; and out of these sufferings we salvage our fragments of happiness (185).

In the late 1940s and early 1950s, Porter's letters and speeches reflect her concern with world politics and the position of the artist in world society. She calls for a continued protection of the humanities and decries blind, fanatical patriotism ("Act of Faith: 4 July 1942"), which she depicts in "Pale Horse, Pale Rider," "The Leaning Tower," and *Ship of Fools*. In "The Future Is Now" (1950) she addresses the fear about the atom bomb but uses the occasion to talk about art. She recalls reading that crawling under a table is as safe as any

other action during a bomb attack and thinks of the artist who lovingly finished such a table for it to serve
beauty and to have a nobler function. In Porter's Opening Speech at the Paris Conference of the International
Exposition of the Arts (1952), she cynically observes
that if the artist's freedom were not threatened it would
not be necessary to cross seas and far countries to
gather together to celebrate it. She defines the artist as
"a kind of synthesis, a sounding board, a mirror, a
sieve, . . . an instrument, . . . a touchstone, . . . a mag-
net, . . . the sacred madman." She warns again against
the unholy alliance of politics and art, and says that the
artist "can play the fool for the love of God and he does
but he shouldn't play the fool for a political party"
(217). She is pleased to point out that the delegation of
Americans (Farrell, Faulkner, Tate, Warren, Wescott, and
Porter) were not chosen on the basis of their political
beliefs (219).

In the Biographical section of *The Collected Essays
and Occasional Writings*, Porter includes essays on Henry
James, Flannery O'Connor, Ford Madox Ford, Stein,
Welty, Tate, T. S. Eliot, Yeats, Joyce, Pound, Jacqueline
Kennedy, Romany Marie, and Joe Gould. Some of these
pieces are slight, adding only minor details to the
known facts of Porter's life, but other pieces are valuable
for their contributions to a more complete knowledge of
Porter's critical philosophy. Porter's essay on Henry
James and the James family, "The Days Before" (1952),
is important for her interpretation of James's definition
of "the problem of the artist," a statement drawn from

THE ESSAYS AND OCCASIONAL WRITINGS

James's preface to *Roderick Hudson*. James had said, "Really, universally, relations stop nowhere, and the exquisite problem of the artist is eternally but to draw, by a geometry of his own, the circle within which they shall happily appear to do so." Porter explains, "While accomplishing this, one has the illusion that destiny is not absolute, it can be arranged, temporized with, persuaded, a little here and there. And once the circle is truly drawn around its contents, it too becomes truth" (248). It is another version of Porter's requirement that the artist shape the chaos of life into a recognizable meaning.

Porter's comments on Gertrude Stein include two reviews of Stein's works ("Everybody Is a Real One" [1927] and "The Wooden Umbrella" [1947]), a parody of Stein's style ("Second Wind" [1928]), and a sequence of correspondence in 1953 with Donald Sutherland ("Ole Woman River"), in which she defends her opinion of Stein. Her three views of Stein include no praise (she depicts Stein as vain and intolerant), but in "The Wooden Umbrella" Porter does give an interesting account of Stein's Paris salon and her influence in Paris. Incidental comments Porter makes about art and the role of the artist are more important than what she has to say about Stein. Once again, Porter speaks of the limits of human understanding. She says, "There are only a few bits of absolute knowledge in the world, people can learn only one or two fundamental facts about each other, the rest is decoration and prejudice" (254). In a letter to Sutherland of 2 June 1953 Porter describes her relationship to Stein and defends herself against the charge of harshness in "The Wooden Umbrella." By way of showing where Stein falls short, in her estimation, she defines art again: "Art does not imitate the shapelessness of life, that is, shapeless, fragmentary life which most individuals see . . . " (278). And she comments again upon the role of the artist: "The Artist must work some order into what I have called somewhere else 'his little handful of chaos,' " a theme she reiterates in a letter to Sutherland a week later. She also defines criticism: "All art comes out of human nature, not just one part, but every cell of it; and so does criticism. You seem to speak as if criticism was some sort of purely scientific apparatus, like a surgeon's kit or a chemistry laboratory, where art, the human organism or tissue, is subjected to a purely impersonal or abstract analysis. There is no such thing as the purely abstract or the purely intellectual, anyway" (280). In a letter to Sutherland of 4 July 1953 she makes an important statement about "the feminine mind," which, she says, resists dogma and categorization and is not at all the disparaged romantic habit of thinking of which Yvor Winters had accused her.

When Porter was living in Salem, Massachusetts, she became interested in the life of Cotton Mather and set about writing his biography. She continued the project during her stay in Bermuda, where she said she finished eleven chapters out of a projected twenty. Although the completed work was announced as forthcoming several times, only three chapters were published, these as separate essays. Porter had no apparent regard for the Puritan pilgrims who settled New England, as her review of George F. Willison's *Saints and Strangers* ("Pull Dick, Pull Devil" [1945]) proves. She says that Willison fails to make his Pilgrims attractive because "their virtues are simply not great enough to overbalance their disturbing lack of charm. And I wish I might never have to hear again that they brought the idea of political and religious freedom to this country. It got in in spite of them; and has had rough going ever since . . . " (144).

The three essays about Mather are nearly as good as her fiction, and like "A Defense of Circe" they contain the same ironic tension as the fiction. Hendrick points out quite rightly that the irony here arises naturally from Porter's subject.[4] "Affectation of Praehiminincies" (1942) is a character study of Mather and the development of his self-importance. "A Goat for Azazel" (1940) is an account of the bewitching of Martha Goodwin, whom Porter calls "the first and most imaginative of all the girls who were to follow her in a blind destructive rebellion against the perversion of life through religion, in the theocratic state" (337). "A Bright Particular Faith" (1934) is an account of Mather's feeling of "brightness" as an assurance from God that his wife would not die. All three essays focus on Mather's self-righteousness and vanity, as he is held up as the most visible representation of the evils of theocracy, a theme Porter also presents in *Ship of Fools*. The puritanical conscience appears in the characters Miriam in "That Tree" and Kennerly in "Hacienda."

Porter's essays on Mexico are especially useful aids in interpreting her stories set in Mexico, since each fictional piece deals with an aspect or stage of the Mexican cultural revolution. "Why I Write about Mexico" (1923) explains Porter's affinity for her "second country," and it shows Porter's sensitivity to the revolution, its causes and aims. She wrote an incisive essay in 1921 called "The Mexican Trinity," in which she identified Land, Oil, and the Church as "the powers that hold this country securely in their grip" (403). She reveals her knowledge of the complex state of Mexican affairs, and it is here that she observes that this revolution, unlike the Russian Revolution, has no writers to carry the cause into the souls of the people. It is a theme she presents effectively in "Flowering Judas" and "Hacienda."

"Leaving the Petate" was written in 1931, after Porter's own idealistic hopes for the revolution had died, and it provides still further insights into the causes of the revolution's failure. She discusses the symbolism of the *petate*, a straw mat on which the Indian sleeps, which became a focal point of the revolution. "Many of the best 1920 revolutionists," Porter wrote, "insisted on smelling of the straw whether they were born on the *petate* or not. It was a mark of the true revolutionary to acknowledge Indian blood, the more the better, to profess Indian points of view, to make, in short, an Indian revolution" (388). But Porter shrewdly points out that

THE ESSAYS AND OCCASIONAL WRITINGS

the Indian will leave the *petate* whenever he gets a chance because he will take "as naturally as any other human or brute being to the delights of kinder living" (389). The difficulty of educating the Indian to the cultural value of his past appears as a theme in "María Concepción" and "Hacienda."

Porter's Preface to *The Itching Parrot*, by J. J. Fernandez Lizárdi, which she translated in 1942 from the Spanish *(El Perequillo Sarniento)*, is both a biographical account of Lizárdi and a sketch of Mexican history relevant to the setting in this picaresque novel. It, along with a letter Porter wrote to the editor of *The Nation* defending her translation, reaffirms her appreciation for eighteenth-century neoclassical prose. "La Conquistadora" (1926) is a biographical sketch of Rosalie Caden Evans, a Texas woman who married an Englishman who owned several haciendas in Mexico during the Díaz regime. Her letters had been published in order to show her side in a controversy over the rights to private ownership, or as Porter says, to "present Mrs. Evans to a presumably outraged Anglo-Saxon world as a martyr to the sacred principles of private ownership of property: to fix her as a symbol of devotion to a holy cause" (417). "The Charmed Life" (1942) is an account of an unnamed aged archaeologist, no doubt William Niven, who was the model for Givens in "María Concepción." "Quetzalcoatl" (1926) is a review of D. H. Lawrence's *The Plumed Serpent*, which Porter says is only incidentally a novel, in spite of the perfection of its form. Although she says that "for sheer magnificence of writing

Lawrence has surpassed himself, she also says that compared to *Sons and Lovers*, this novel is a catastrophe. This review balances her later devastating attack on Lawrence and *Lady Chatterley's Lover* ("A Wreath for the Gamekeeper").

The category "On Writing" that Porter added to *The Collected Essays* includes two pieces from the "Personal and Particular" category in *The Days Before*. In "My First Speech" (1934) she continues to argue for the private life of the author; she again cites legend and memory as sources for the writer but adds a third source: the present explanation for the memory and the legend, that is, the recreation of it. She says that "all this is working at once in my mind, in a confusion of dimensions" (433). In a letter to Eugene Pressly two years later ("Notes on Writing") she said, "This constant exercise of memory seems to be the chief occupation of my mind, and all my experience seems to be simply memory, with continuity, marginal notes, constant revision and comparison of one thing with another. Now and again thousands of memories converge, harmonize, arrange themselves around a central idea in a coherent form, and I write a story" (449). Her comments in both the speech and this letter help to explain the viewpoint of "The Old Order" and "Old Mortality" in particular. In the speech Porter goes on to describe her purpose and method as artist: "to give a true testimony it is necessary to know and remember what I was, what I felt, and what I knew then, and not confuse it with what I know or think I know now. So I shall try to tell the

THE ESSAYS AND OCCASIONAL WRITINGS

truth, but the result will be fiction. I shall not be at all surprised at this result: it is what I mean to do; it is, to my way of thinking, the way fiction is made" (433). Her speech was in a way prophetic. She said, "Artists do not always create a pleasant world, because that is not their business. If they do that, you will be right not to trust them in anything" (439). She might have been defending herself against some of the public reaction to *Ship of Fools* nearly thirty years later.

Although much of Porter's commentary on writing gives insight into her purpose and method, no single piece does so as well as " 'Noon Wine': The Sources." Citing again the three sources for the writer she identified in "My First Speech," she now adds a fourth, the process of discovery when the writer is asked, as she was, "to trace his clues to their sources and to expose the roots of his work in his most secret and private life" (467). She explores the genesis of "Noon Wine" brilliantly and carefully, examining the memory and culling out the real events that fed into it.[5]

While many of the uncollected reviews shed additional light on Porter's aesthetic and worldview, two long pieces, *Outline of Mexican Popular Arts and Crafts* (1922) and *The Never-Ending Wrong* (1977), deserve particular attention. The *Outline*, written to accompany an art exhibit to the United States, shows Porter's knowledge and appreciation of Mexican cultural history. Porter's ironic tone is present as she exalts the primitive folk art over the civilized. Her description of her aim in the *Outline* explains much of the theme of "María Concepción." She has intended to present, she says, "in its human aspect, this profound and touching expressing of a very old race, surviving and persisting in its devotion to ancient laws with a steadfastness that is an anachronism in this fluctuating age. These pages will perhaps help to explain many things to those who will see, for the first time, examples of this art extending over a period of at least fifteen centuries" (56).

Porter took notes for *The Never-Ending Wrong* during the 1920s when she followed the "strange history" of the Italian emigrants Nicola Sacco and Bartolomeo Vanzetti, who were accused of a brutal murder and the robbery of a payroll truck in South Braintree, Massachusetts, April 15, 1920. Porter was among those who marched and were arrested in Boston and kept vigil during the execution of the pair. While she says that even in 1977 she is not certain of their guilt or innocence, she declares without equivocation that the case was "one of the important turning points in the history of this country; not the cause, but the symptom of a change so deep and so sinister in the whole point of view and direction of this people as a nation" (38). Although she deplores the exploitation of the cause by the Communists, she compares the trial of Sacco and Vanzetti to those of Jesus and Joan of Arc, the Salem witchcraft trials of the seventeenth century, and the Moscow trials of 1937, during which the State destroyed all the founders of the 1924 Soviet Revolution. Her summary of this event in Boston is in many respects a summary of her view of humanity; she calls it "one of the most portentous in the long death of civilization made by Europeans in the Western World, in the millenial upheaval which brings almost every possible change but one—the two nearly matched forces of human nature, the will to give life and the will to destroy it" (48).

Taken altogether, Porter's nonfictional works indeed do seem to confirm the shape and direction of her fiction. They mirror the structure and tone of the fiction while they reveal considerable detail about her comprehensive conception of the world and identify those writers who inspired her and those works which provided stylistic models for her developing craft. Over the course of more than fifty years, Porter wove into the nonfiction the aesthetic theory that underlies the fiction and the artistic standards to which she aspired. The student and admirer of Porter's work has in the nonfiction another rich display of Porter's extraordinary skill and an important critical apparatus to apply to her fiction.

Notes

1. See, for example, "It is Hard to Stand in the Middle" (40) and "From the Notebooks: Yeats, Joyce, Eliot, Pound" (298).

2. See Marjorie Ryan, "*Dubliners* and the Stories of Katherine Anne Porter," *American Literature* 31 (Jan. 1960): 464–73.

3. See Glenway Wescott, "Katherine Anne Porter Personally," *Images of Truth* (New York: Harper and Row, 1962) 36.

4. George Hendrick, *Katherine Anne Porter* (New York: Twayne, 1965) 150.

5. For further exploration into sources for characters in the story, see Joan Givner, *Katherine Anne Porter: A Life* (New York: Simon and Schuster, 1982) 73–75.

BIBLIOGRAPHY

I. Books by Katherine Anne Porter

My Chinese Marriage. (Signed "M. T. F.") New York: Duffield, 1921.

Outline of Mexican Popular Arts and Crafts. [Los Angeles: Young and McCallister], 1922.

What Price Marriage? New York: J. H. Sears, [1927]. Compiled with an introduction (signed "Hamblen Sears") by Porter.

Flowering Judas and Other Stories. New York: Harcourt, Brace, 1930. Contents: "María Concepción," "Magic," "Rope," "He," "The Jilting of Granny Weatherall," "Flowering Judas."

Katherine Anne Porter's French Song-Book. [Paris]: Harrison of Paris, 1933.

Hacienda. [New York]: Harrison of Paris, 1934.

Flowering Judas and Other Stories. New York: Harcourt, Brace, 1935. London: Cape, 1936. Contents: The 1930 edition, "Theft," "The Cracked Looking-Glass," "Hacienda." 1935 edition reprinted in 1940 by Modern Library with a new introduction by the author.

Noon Wine. Detroit: Schuman's, 1937.

Pale Horse, Pale Rider: Three Short Novels. New York: Harcourt, Brace, 1939. London: Cape, 1939. Contents: "Old Mortality," "Noon Wine," "Pale Horse, Pale Rider." Reprinted by Modern Library in 1949.

The Itching Parrot. A translation of *El Perequillo Sarniento,* by José Joaquín Lizárdi. Garden City, New York: Doubleday, 1942.

The Leaning Tower and Other Stories. New York: Harcourt, Brace, 1944. London: Cape, 1945. Contents: "The Source," "The Witness," "The Circus," "The Old Order," "The Last

Leaf," "The Grave," "The Downward Path to Wisdom," "A Day's Work," and "The Leaning Tower."

The Days Before. New York: Harcourt, Brace, 1952. Contents: "The Days Before," "On a Criticism of Thomas Hardy," "Gertrude Stein: Three Views," "Reflections on Willa Cather," " 'It is Hard to Stand in the Middle,' " "The Art of Katherine Mansfield," "Orpheus in Purgatory," "The Laughing Heat of the Sun," "Eudora Welty and *A Curtain of Green*," "Homage to Ford Madox Ford," "Virginia Woolf," "E. M. Forster," "Three Statements about Writing," "No Plot, My Dear, No Story," "The Flower of Flowers," "Portrait: Old South," "Audubon's Happy Land," "A House of My Own," "The Necessary Enemy," " 'Marriage Is Belonging,' " "American Statement: 4 July 1942," "The Future Is Now," "Notes on the Life and Death of a Hero," "Why I Write about Mexico," "Leaving the Petate," "The Mexican Trinity," "La Conquistadora," "Quetzalcoatl," "The Charmed Life."

A Defense of Circe. New York: Harcourt, Brace, 1955.

The Old Order: Stories of the South. New York: Harcourt, Brace, 1955. Contents: "The Old Order," "The Jilting of Granny Weatherall," "He," "Magic," and "Old Mortality."

Ship of Fools. Boston and Toronto: Little, Brown/Atlantic Monthly, 1962. London: Secker and Warburg, 1962.

The Collected Stories of Katherine Anne Porter. London: Cape, 1964. Contents: *Flowering Judas and Other Stories* (1935); *Pale Horse, Pale Rider: Three Short Novels;* and *The Leaning Tower and Other Stories.*

The Collected Stories of Katherine Anne Porter. New York: Harcourt, Brace & World, 1965. London: Cape, 1967. Augmented text, includes also "The Martyr," "Virgin Violeta," and "Holiday."

BIBLIOGRAPHY

A Christmas Story. New York: Delacorte Press, 1967.

The Collected Essays and Occasional Writings of Katherine Anne Porter. New York: Delacorte Press, 1970. Contents: All of *The Days Before;* "A Wreath for the Gamekeeper," "On Christopher Sykes," "Max Beerbohm," "Eleanor Clark," "The Winged Skull," "On Modern Fiction," "A Little Incident in the Rue de l'Odeon," "A Letter to Sylvia Beach," "Letters to a Nephew," "Dylan Thomas," "A Defense of Circe," "Pull Dick, Pull Devil," "A Note on Pierre-Joseph Redoute," "A Letter to the Editor of the *Village Voice,*" "A Letter to the Editor of *The Saturday Review of Literature,*" "Opening Speech at Paris Conference, 1951," "Remarks on the Agenda," "A Letter to the Editor of *The Yale Review,*" "A Letter to the Editor of the *Washington Post,*" "Speech of Acceptance"; "Ole Woman River," "A Sprig of Mint for Allen," "On First Meeting T. S. Eliot," "Flannery O'Connor at Home," "From the Notebooks: Yeats, Joyce, Eliot, Pound," "Romany Marie, Joe Gould—Two Legends Come to Life," "Jacqueline Kennedy," "Miss Porter Adds a Comment," "The Fiesta of Guadalupe," "My First Speech," "Notes on Writing," "On Writing," " 'Noon Wine': The Sources"; Poems: "Enchanted," "Two Songs from Mexico," "Little Requiem," "Winter Burial," "Anniversary in a Country Cemetery," "November in Windham," "After a Long Journey," "Measures for Song and Dance."

The Never-Ending Wrong. Boston: Atlantic-Little, Brown, 1977.

II.   Selected Uncollected Writings

"Adventures of Hadji: A Tale of a Turkish Coffee-House, retold by Katherine Anne Porter." *Asia* 20 (1920): 683–84.

"The Shattered Star." *Everyland* Jan. 1920: 422–23.

BIBLIOGRAPHY

"The Faithful Princess." *Everyland* Feb. 1920: 42–43.

"The Magic Earring." *Everyland* Mar. 1920: 86–87.

"Corridos." *Survey* 52 (1924): 157–59.

"From a Mexican Painter's Notebooks." *Arts* 7 (1925): 21–23.

"Mr. George on The Woman Problem." *New York Herald Tribune Books* 29 Nov. 1925: 11.

"Children and Art." *Nation* 124 (1927): 233–34.

[Comment on "Flowering Judas"]. *This Is My Best*, ed. Whit Burnett. New York: The Dial Press, 1942. 539–40.

"Introduction." *Fiesta in November*, ed. A. Flores and D. Poore. Boston: Houghton Mifflin Co., 1942.

"The Spivvleton Mystery." *Ladies Home Journal* 88 (1971): 74–75.

"Recollection of Rome." *Travel and Leisure* (Jan. 1974): 4–.

"You Are What You Read." *Vogue* 164 (Oct. 1974): 248.

"Notes on the Texas I Remember." *The Atlantic* 235.3 (Mar. 1975): 102–06.

III.   Bibliographies and Checklists

Bixby, George. "Katherine Anne Porter: A Bibliographical Checklist." *American Book Collector* 1.6 (1980): 19–33. A descriptive bibliography of the first editions of Porter's books and of selected books in which works by Porter are included.

Givner, Joan, Jane DeMouy, and Ruth M. Alvarez. "Katherine Anne Porter." *American Women Writers: A Critical Reference Guide from Colonial Times to the Present*, ed. Lina Mainiero. New York: Frederick Ungar, 1979. 201–31. A bibliographical essay that identifies the important primary materials and evaluates the biographical and critical studies.

BIBLIOGRAPHY

Kiernan, Robert F. *Katherine Anne Porter and Carson McCullers: A Reference Guide.* Boston: G. K. Hall, 1976. Useful abstracts of criticism from 1924–74.

Schwartz, Edward. "Katherine Anne Porter: A Critical Bibliography." With an introduction by Robert Penn Warren. *Bulletin of the New York Public Library* 57 (May 1953): 211–47. Rpt. *Katherine Anne Porter: A Critical Bibliography.* Folcroft, PA: Folcroft Press, 1969. An annotated listing of Porter's works and reviews with criticism of the works,.

Waldrip, Louise and Shirley Ann Bauer. *A Bibliography of the Works of Katherine Anne Porter* and *A Bibliography of the Criticism of the Works of Katherine Anne Porter.* Metuchen, NJ: The Scarecrow Press, 1969.

IV. Biographies

Givner, Joan. *Katherine Anne Porter: A Life.* New York: Simon and Schuster, 1982. A carefully researched study which fills in the gaps in what was previously known about Porter's life.

Lopez, Enrique Hank. *Conversations with Katherine Anne Porter: Refugee from Indian Creek.* Boston: Little, Brown, 1981. A piecing together of Porter's life from taped conversations with the author and from previously published works on Porter; suffers from inaccuracies of details but nevertheless valuable for some new material.

V. Critical Books

DeMouy, Jane Krause. *Katherine Anne Porter's Women: The Eye of Her Fiction.* Austin: University of Texas Press, 1983. An analysis of the major works of the canon (with the exception of "Noon Wine" and "The Leaning Tower"), from a feminist perspective.

Emmons, Winfred S. *Katherine Anne Porter: The Regional Stories.* Southwest Writers Series, No. 6. Austin, TX: Steck-Vaughn, 1967. A monograph focusing on the stories set in Texas: "The Old Order," "Old Mortality," "Noon Wine," "Holiday," "He."

Hardy, John Edward. *Katherine Anne Porter.* New York: Frederick Ungar, 1973. A useful interpretation of some stories but contains inaccurate biographical information.

Hendrick, George. *Katherine Anne Porter.* New York: Twayne, 1965. A thorough and well-written overview.

Liberman, M. M. *Katherine Anne Porter's Fiction.* Detroit: Wayne State University Press, 1971. An excellent series of essays on "Old Mortality," "Noon Wine," "The Leaning Tower," "María Concepción," "Holiday," "Flowering Judas," "He," and *Ship of Fools.*

Mooney, Harry J., Jr. *The Fiction and Criticism of Katherine Anne Porter.* Critical Essays in Modern Literature. Pittsburgh: University of Pittsburgh Press, 1957; rev., 1962. A tracing through the short fiction and *Ship of Fools* of what Mooney sees as Porter's abiding faith in humanity.

Nance, William L. *Katherine Anne Porter and the Art of Rejection.* Chapel Hill: University of North Carolina Press, 1964. An analysis of the stories and *Ship of Fools* as variations on a theme of escape.

Unrue, Darlene Harbour. *Truth and Vision in Katherine Anne Porter's Fiction.* Athens: University of Georgia Press, 1985. An interpretation of the canon by application of Porter's worldview, gleaned from essays and unpublished letters.

West, Ray B., Jr. *Katherine Anne Porter.* University of Minnesota Pamphlets on American Writers, No. 28. Minneapolis: Uni-

BIBLIOGRAPHY

versity of Minnesota Press, 1963. A worthwhile but narrow reading of the canon, focusing on symbols as thematic indicators in a work.

VI.   Collections of Interviews and Essays

Givner, Joan. *Katherine Anne Porter: Conversations.* Jackson: University Press of Mississippi, 1987. A gathering of published interviews and panel discussions 1916–1976, arranged chronologically; includes an introduction by Givner.

Hartley, Lodwick and George Core, eds. *Katherine Anne Porter: A Critical Symposium.* Athens: University of Georgia Press, 1969. An excellent gathering of biographical and critical pieces on Porter and her work.

Warren, Robert Penn, ed. *Katherine Anne Porter: A Collection of Critical Essays.* Twentieth Century Views Series. Englewood Cliffs, NJ: Prentice-Hall, 1979. A valuable collection of essays and reviews, nearly one-half of which focus on the controversy over *Ship of Fools;* includes an introduction by Warren.

VII.   Sections of Books

Auchincloss, Louis. "Katherine Anne Porter." In *Pioneers and Caretakers: A Study of Nine American Women Novelists.* Minneapolis: University of Minnesota Press, 1965. 136–51. An analysis of the relationship of "Old Mortality," "Pale Horse, Pale Rider," "Noon Wine," and "The Leaning Tower" to *Ship of Fools.*

Hoffman, Frederick J. *The Art of Southern Fiction: A Study of Some Modern Novelists.* Carbondale and Edwardsville:

BIBLIOGRAPHY

Southern Illinois University Press, 1967. 39–50. An examination of Porter's disposition toward the past in the Miranda stories; analyses of "Noon Wine" and *Ship of Fools*.

Joselyn, Sister M. "Animal Imagery in Katherine Anne Porter's Fiction." In *Myth and Symbol: Critical Approaches and Applications*, ed. Bernice Slote. Lincoln: University of Nebraska Press, 1963. 101–15. A classification of the animal imagery in "Flowering Judas," "Pale Horse, Pale Rider," "The Leaning Tower," "The Circus," "The Downward Path to Wisdom," and *Ship of Fools* according to its function.

Wescott, Glenway. "Katherine Anne Porter Personally." In *Images of Truth: Remembrances and Criticism*. New York: Harper and Row, 1962. 25–58. Rpt. in Hartley and Core 24–48; Warren, *A Collection of Critical Essays* 36–58. A rich remembrance of a friendship with Porter; includes especially valuable analyses of "Noon Wine," "Pale Horse, Pale Rider," and *Ship of Fools*.

VIII.   Critical Articles about Porter

Brooks, Cleanth. "On 'The Grave.' " *Yale Review* 55 (1966): 175–79. Rpt. in Hartley and Core 115–19; Warren, *A Collection of Critical Essays* 112–16. A succinct interpretation of the story as a rite of initiation grounded in a social and philosophical context.

Core, George. "The Best Residuum of Truth." *Georgia Review* 20 (1966): 278–91. Rpt. with revisions in Hartley and Core 149–58. A valuable interpretation of "Holiday" as a pastoral story in which the structure provides significant clues to the meaning.

Curley, Daniel. "Treasure in 'The Grave.' " *Modern Fiction Studies* 9 (1963): 377–84. An identification of the story's fun-

BIBLIOGRAPHY

damental concept as the mind of the writer being the grave of the past.

Gottfried, Leon. "Death's Other Kingdom: Dantesque and Theological Symbolism in 'Flowering Judas.' " *PMLA* 84 (1969): 112–24. A placing of "Flowering Judas" in the ironic mode of Dante, Milton, and Eliot, in which an elaborate system of religious allusions functions.

Gross, Beverly. "The Poetic Narrative: A Reading of 'Flowering Judas.' " *Style* 2 (Spring 1968): 129–39. A stylistic study of the poetic qualities in the story's language and form.

Hamovitch, Mitzi Berger. "Today and Yesterday: Letters from Katherine Anne Porter." *The Centennial Review* 27 (Fall 1983): 278–87. An illustration of Porter's worldview with excerpts from her correspondence with *The Hound & Horn*.

Hartley, Lodwick. "Dark Voyagers: A Study of Katherine Anne Porter's *Ship of Fools*." *University Review* 30 (1963): 83–94. Rpt. in Hartley and Core 211–26. An interpretation of *Ship of Fools* as a study of the terrible failure of western man.

Heilman, Robert B. "*Ship of Fools*: Notes on Style." *Four Quarters* 12 (Nov. 1962): 46–55. Rpt. in Hartley and Core 197–210. A thorough analysis of the elements of style in *Ship of Fools*, as representative of style in the canon; sees Porter's style as having strong affiliations with that of Austen and Eliot.

Hertz, Robert N. "Sebastian Brant and Porter's *Ship of Fools*." *The Midwest Quarterly* 6 (1965): 389–401. A study of the differences between Brant's work and Porter's; leads to a useful interpretation of *Ship of Fools*.

Johnson, James William. "Another Look at Katherine Anne Porter." *Virginia Quarterly Review* 36 (1960): 598–613. Rpt. in Hartley and Core 83–96. An interpretation of the stories by

BIBLIOGRAPHY

the application of a "logos" produced by the recurring themes in the fiction.

Kaplan, Charles. "True Witness: Katherine Anne Porter." *Colorado Quarterly* 7 (Winter 1959): 319–27. A chronological organization of the Miranda stories with valuable remarks on "The Circus."

Kirkpatrick, Smith. *"Ship of Fools."* *Sewanee Review* 71 (1963): 93–98. Rpt. in Warren, *A Collection of Critical Essays,* 165–69. An examination of the mask motif that leads to the novel's universal themes.

Liberman, M. M. "The Responsibility of the Novelist: The Critical Reception of *Ship of Fools.*" *Criticism* 8 (1966): 377–88. Rpt. Warren, *A Collection of Critical Essays* 179–89. A defense of *Ship of Fools* which defines its genre as apologue.

———. "Some Observations on the Genesis of *Ship of Fools*: A Letter From Katherine Anne Porter." *PMLA* 73 (1968): 136–37. An examination of a letter from Porter to Malcolm Cowley of 25 September 1931 which mentions images that appear in "The Leaning Tower" and *Ship of Fools.*

Moddelmog, Debra A. "Narrative Irony and Hidden Motivations in Katherine Anne Porter's 'He.' " *Modern Fiction Studies* 28 (Autumn 1982): 405–13. An interpretation that relies on Mrs. Whipple's death wish for her retarded son, backed up with psychoanalytical studies.

Perry, Robert L. "Porter's 'Hacienda' and the Theme of Change." *Midwest Quarterly* 6 (Summer 1965): 403–15. A detailed illustration of the motif that provides the index to the work's most important theme.

Praeger, Leonard. "Getting and Spending: Porter's 'Theft.' " *Perspective* 11 (1960): 230–34. A careful explication of the story, centering on the symbolism of the purse and the technique of recalling the past.

BIBLIOGRAPHY

Ryan, Marjorie. "Dubliners and the Stories of Katherine Anne Porter." *American Literature* 31 (Jan. 1960): 464–73. An identification, in some of Porter's stories, of the moral paralysis that Joyce's stories uncover; in other Porter stories a pointing out of Joyce's technique of allowing meaning to rest in action rather than symbol.

Schorer, Mark. "We're All on the Passenger List." *New York Times* 1 Apr. 1962: 1, 5. Rpt. in Warren, *A Collection of Critical Essays* 130–33. Praise for *Ship of Fools*, which he places among the greatest novels of the past hundred years.

Schwartz, Edward G. "The Fictions of Memory." *Southwest Review* 45 (Summer 1960): 204–15. Rpt. in Hartley and Core 67–82. An exposition of the "moral drama" in the stories, an initiation theme that focuses on the changing of orders as a metaphor for the changing responsibilities and perspectives in human life.

_____. "The Way of Dissent: Katherine Anne Porter's Critical Position." *Western Humanities Review* 8 (Spring 1954): 119–30. Rpt. in Hartley and Core 169–82; Warren, *A Collection of Critical Essays* 82–92. An examination of Porter's essays that reveal her aesthetic principles and general philosophical position; sees her artistic preoccupation with truth-telling as essentially religious.

Solotaroff, Theodore. "*Ship of Fools* and the Critics." *Commentary* 34 (1962): 277–86. Rpt. in Warren, *A Collection of Critical Essays* 134–49. An attack on *Ship of Fools* as stagnant and repetitive; sees the novel as little more than statement of misanthropy presented with clever technique.

Stein, William Bysshe. " 'Theft': Porter's Politics of Modern Love." *Perspective* 11 (Winter 1960): 223–28. An interpretation of the story as the inevitable consequence of the betrayal of the holistic ideal of Christian love.

BIBLIOGRAPHY

Tate, Allen. "A New Star." *Nation* 131 (Oct. 1930): 352–53. A review of *Flowering Judas and Other Stories* (1930) in which Porter is seen as more in tune with European fiction than the "thinner" American variety.

Walsh, Thomas F. "Deep Similarities in 'Noon Wine.' " *Mosaic* 9 (1975): 83–91. A thematic analysis based on the concept of the double as interpreted by Otto Rank.

———. "The Dream's Self in 'Pale Horse, Pale Rider.' " *Wascana Review* 14.2 (Fall 1979): 61–79. A detailed examination of the story's five dreams in which the opening dream is seen as establishing the ironic pattern of the story; relies on R. D. Laing's *The Divided Self* for support.

———. "The Making of 'Flowering Judas.' " *Journal of Modern Literature* 12 (Mar. 1985): 109–30. A carefully researched and documented study which distinguishes between the real persons and events that inspired the story and Porter's alterations for artistic reasons.

———. "Miranda's Ghost in 'Old Mortality.' " *College Literature* 6 (1979–1980): 57–63. A study of Aunt Amy as Miranda's "ghost" who could reveal truths about the hidden, paradoxical patterns of human behavior.

———. "The 'Noon Wine' Devils." *The Georgia Review* 22 (Spring 1968): 90–96. An identification of the Faustian pattern in "Noon Wine," relying on Porter's excerpts from the unfinished biography of Cotton Mather and Benet's "The Devil and Daniel Webster" as the modern model of the pattern.

———. "Xochitl: Katherine Anne Porter's Changing Goddess." *American Literature* 52 (1980): 183–93. A valuable study of the influence of ancient Mayan and Aztec myths on Porter's Mexican fiction.

BIBLIOGRAPHY

Warren, Robert Penn. "Katherine Anne Porter (Irony with a Center)." *The Kenyon Review* 4 (1942): 29–42. Rpt. in Hartley and Core 51–66; Warren, *A Collection of Critical Essays* 93–108. A study of paradox, as the essential element in Porter's irony, in "Flowering Judas," "Old Mortality," "Noon Wine," and "The Cracked Looking-Glass."

Welty, Eudora. "The Eye of the Story." *Yale Review* 55 (Winter 1966): 265–74. Rpt. in Hartley and Core, 103–12; Warren, *A Collection of Critical Essays* 72–80. An exposition of Porter's slight reliance on the physical world in contrast to the rich interior settings; considers imagery, anger, "robust" despair, and the sense of urgency as important elements in the fiction.

Wiesenfarth, Brother Joseph. "Illusion and Allusion: Reflections in 'The Cracked Looking-Glass.' " *Four Quarters* 12 (1962): 30–37. Rpt. in Hartley and Core, 139–48. An explanation of the story as the complex action of a woman's making her life meaningful; a comparison with the mirror symbols in *Ulysses* and "The Lady of Shalott."

_____. "Internal Opposition in Porter's 'Granny Weatherall.' " *Critique* 11 (1969): 47–55. A comparison of the theme of order versus disorder in "The Source" and "The Jilting of Granny Weatherall."

_____. "The Structure of Katherine Anne Porter's 'Theft.' " *Cithara* 10 (May 1971): 64–71. A reading of the story as a "whodunit" with two epiphanies, one of loss and one of guilt, and as a story about loss of innocence.

Wilson, Edmund. "Katherine Anne Porter." *New Yorker* 20 (Sept. 1944): 64–66. Rpt. in *Classics and Commercials: A Literary Chronicle of the Forties.* New York: Farrar, Strauss, 1950. 219–23; Warren, *A Collection of Critical Essays* 126–29. A classification of the stories into three groups: family life, pictures of foreign parts, and stories about women; sees the stories as defying formulaic interpretation.

IX. Interviews and Discussions

Bode, Winston. "Miss Porter on Writers and Writing." *The Texas Observer* 31 Oct. 1958: 6–7.

Doblier, Maurice. "I've Had a Good Run for My Money." *New York Herald Tribune Books* 1 Apr. 1962: 3, 11.

Dolan, Mary Anne. "Almost Since Chaucer with Miss Porter." *Washington Star* 11 May 1975: A1, A6.

Dorsey, John. "Katherine Anne Porter on. . . . " *Baltimore Sun Magazine* 26 Oct. 1969: 16.

From Invitation to Learning, a series of radio broadcasts: "Alice in Wonderland," in *The New Invitation to Learning,* edited by Mark Van Doren. New York: New Home Library, 1942. A discussion with Bertrand Russell and Van Doren. 208–20. "Moll Flanders," in *The Invitation to Learning,* edited by Huntington Cairns, Allen Tate, and Mark Van Doren. New York: New Home Library, 1942. With the editors. 137–51. "The Turn of the Screw," in *The New Invitation to Learning.* With Tate and Van Doren. 223–35.

Janeway, Elizabeth. "For Katherine Anne Porter, *Ship of Fools* Was a Lively Twenty-Two Year Voyage." *New York Times Book Review* 1 Apr. 1962: 4–5.

Lopez, Hank. "A Country and Some People I Love." *Harper's* 231 (Sept. 1965): 58. Rpt. in Warren, *A Collection of Critical Essays* 19–35.

Newquist, Roy. "An Interview with Katherine Anne Porter." *McCall's* 92 (Aug. 1965): 88.

"Recent Southern Fiction: A Panel Discussion." *Bulletin of Wesleyan College* 41 (Jan. 1961): 1–6.

BIBLIOGRAPHY

Ruoff, James. "Katherine Anne Porter Comes to Kansas." *The Midwest Quarterly* 4 (1963): 205–34.

"Some Important Authors Speak for Themselves." *New York Herald Tribune Books* 12 Oct. 1952: 8.

Thompson, Barbara. "The Art of Fiction XXIX—Katherine Anne Porter: An Interview." *Paris Review,* No. 29 (1963): 87–114. Rpt. in *Writers at Work: The Paris Review Interviews.* New York: The Viking Press, 1963. 137–63; Hartley and Core 3–23.

Van Gelder, Robert. "Katherine Anne Porter at Work." *The New York Times Book Review* 14 Apr. 1940: 20.

Winston, Archer. "Presenting the Portrait of an Artist." *The New York Post* 6 May 1937: 17.

INDEX

This index does not include references to material in the notes.

INDEX

INDEX

INDEX

INDEX

INDEX

INDEX

INDEX

INDEX